# FIGHT BACK

## END THE CYCLES OF ANXIETY AND DEPRESSION

MIKE OGLESBEE

**BALBOA**.PRESS

A DIVISION OF HAY HOUSE

Balboa Press books may be ordered through booksellers or by contacting:

Balboa Press
A Division of Hay House
1663 Liberty Drive
Bloomington, IN 47403
www.balboapress.com
1 (877) 407-4847

ISBN: 978-1-9822-4645-7 (sc)
ISBN: 978-1-9822-4647-1 (hc)
ISBN: 978-1-9822-4646-4 (e)

Library of Congress Control Number: 2020906945

Printed in the United States of America.

Balboa Press rev. date: 07/09/2020

*To the most loving, kind, and supportive woman I've ever had the honor and pleasure of knowing, my wife, Shannon Oglesbee*

# CONTENTS

Introduction ........................................................................................ xi

## PART I. UNDERSTANDING THE MIND

**CHAPTER 1**  Measuring and Tracking Anxiety and Depression ........1

Burns Anxiety Inventory .............................................................4

Burns Depression Checklist ......................................................5

**CHAPTER 2**  The Theory of Mind ........................................................7

The Conscious and Subconscious Mind ................................8

The Language of the Subconscious Mind ...........................11

Event + Internal Representation = Experience ..................12

The Critical Mind .....................................................................14

The Primitive Mind ..................................................................15

Right versus Left Brain ...........................................................16

Neural Pathways .......................................................................18

How the Subconscious Mind Learns ...................................19

**CHAPTER 3**  Symptoms versus Problems .........................................21

Defense Mechanisms ...............................................................22

Pain versus Pleasure Principle ..............................................25

The Fear Factor .........................................................................27

## PART II. A NEW FOUNDATION

**CHAPTER 4**  Laying the Groundwork ...............................................33

Mental Training ........................................................................35

The Impact of Your Words .....................................................40

The Impact of Your Environment ........................................42

Control and Faith .....................................................................44

**CHAPTER 5**  The Model of Power .......................................................49

Truth ...........................................................................55

**CHAPTER 6**  Setting Growth Goals ..........................................59

Process versus Result Orientation ........................................62

**CHAPTER 7**  The Process of Growth ........................................67

The Terror Barrier ..................................................... 68

One Step at a Time .................................................................71

**CHAPTER 8**  Acceptance ...........................................................73

Expectation versus Reality ....................................................78

Shifting Your Focus .................................................................79

Putting the Process into Practice ..........................................81

# PART III. THE TOOLS AND TECHNIQUES

**CHAPTER 9**  Changing Your Experiences ...............................85

The Model of Human Experience ...........................................85

**CHAPTER 10** Self-Management ...................................................91

Needs versus Wants .................................................................92

Discernment and Self-Regulation ..........................................93

Effective Decision Making ..................................................... 96

"Should" Statements, Guilt, and Shame .............................. 99

Identifying with Problems......................................................103

Putting Discernment into Practice .......................................107

**CHAPTER 11** Resolving Problems...............................................109

Part I: Problem ......................................................................110

Part II: Truth ........................................................................ 114

Part III: Insight......................................................................114

Part IV: Responsibility...........................................................116

Part I: Problem ........................................................ 118
Part II: Truth ........................................................ 120
Part III: Insight........................................................ 120
Part IV: Responsibility........................................................121

**CHAPTER 12** Overcoming Intrusive Thoughts.................................... 123

Fear-Based Intrusive Thoughts............................................131

**CHAPTER 13** Healing Core Issues........................................................139

Mirror Technique................................................................146
Meditation ........................................................150
Diet and Exercise................................................................152
Ending the Cycles................................................................153

Bibliography........................................................155
About the Author........................................................157

# INTRODUCTION

In 2011, I opened Maximized Mind, LLC, in Myrtle Beach, South Carolina, where I specialize in helping adults overcome anxiety and depression using the most effective tools and techniques that psychology and the field of self-help have to offer, including NLP coaching, hypnotherapy, and other forms of traditional and alternative therapeutic modalities. I have helped people throughout the world overcome anxiety and depression by helping them replace the subconscious programs within them that cause these issues and teach them how to use their conscious minds in a more effective way to gain balanced and peaceful lives. I firmly believe the key to overcoming anxiety and depression is empowerment or, more importantly, self-empowerment. Empowerment comes through knowledge, and knowledge about the self becomes self-empowerment. Therefore, I devote much of my time teaching my clients how to understand their subconscious programs behind the challenges they are experiencing, why they are facing them, and how to safely and effectively remove and replace them with healthy ones that are more effective. It may sound complicated, but after reading this book, you will have a better understanding of subconscious programs as well as the process of replacing them.

Since childhood, I've battled severe anxiety and depression. For me, nothing ever seemed to work. I tried everything I knew of, including medications, reading self-help books, and attending counseling several times. I seemed to be immune to everything that worked for everyone else, that I was somehow different and nothing could help someone as unique and diverse as I am. I had suicidal tendencies as a teenager and throughout my early thirties, developed OCDs, disassociated from my body at times, and even hallucinated from extreme anxiety. I've experienced uncontrollable panic attacks and excruciating pain in my chest and body. I've caused damage to my life as well as others'. I've hurt people through my actions and done some rather messed-up things. I've created dysfunction in almost every area of my life at times. I messed up at times because I was messed up. I hated life for over thirty years because I was always in pain and suffering. I was angry, bitter, and resentful, but I never knew why. For me, life was a struggle.

It wasn't until I began to learn about the subconscious mind and how to reprogram it effectively that I began to see and experience actual lasting results in my life. I began to experience what it felt like to go long periods without feeling empty and worthless inside. I started giving and receiving true genuine love for others and myself. The void within began to transform into passion and excitement. The weight of the world lifted, and I finally felt a real sense of freedom in my mind. I learned to turn my inner critic into an amazing inner coach, and my life took on greater meaning. I no longer sabotaged all the good things in my life, and I had a reason to chase my dreams. I finally began to live my life on my terms, the way I always wanted. It was no longer a daily struggle. I was motivated and inspired to make something of myself for me, not to gain acceptance and value from and through others who seemed to dictate my life with their views and opinions. I became authentic, and I have loved living life since.

Did this take work? Yes. Do I still do the work? Yes. Some association from my past that I didn't work through because I wasn't aware of it earlier in my self-healing process may occasionally trigger an old program. This requires me to acknowledge and resolve it within my conscious and subconscious mind. I've never allowed myself to forget the pain and suffering of going through life with debilitating anxiety and depression, for it motivates me to continue working on myself to become better and stronger. I call this simple maintenance. Now that I have the tools and understanding of how and why these things affect me, I can quickly work through them in minimum time with minimum effort. I'm very grateful for my experiences with anxiety and depression because, through my transformation, I am now able to help others heal effectively and achieve similar results in their lives, and that's the greatest gift I've ever received.

Throughout my years of helping people overcome anxiety and depression, I have learned that the most powerful way to do this is through knowledge, understanding, and practicality. I have found my clients' results are much more effective, long lasting, and more practical when they understand what they are going through and why these things are happening to them. It's like the old proverb "Give a man a fish, and you'll feed him for a day; teach a man to fish, and you'll feed him for a lifetime." My job is not to help people but to empower them to help themselves. I believe that you can only help those who help themselves. It's impossible to do the work for someone else. Teaching them how to do it for themselves is when the healing can begin to happen.

Many people do their best to fight anxiety and depression but typically fail to get them under control. The first step in overcoming anxiety and depression is to learn about and begin to understand how the mind works, which will help you more fully understand the concepts and teachings in this book and why each is so important to implement to overcome them once and for all. Part I is designed to teach and empower you with this knowledge and understanding. Since you will be working with your mind to overcome anxiety and depression, you must know and understand how the mind works. This is where most people fall short in their journey to healing. Several things I teach in this book may be new to you, things that you may not have ever heard before, especially when it comes to the subconscious mind. I challenge you to read this with a curious and open mind so you can allow yourself a new opportunity to overcome debilitating anxiety and depression in your life—for good.

In Part II, I will teach you how to create and lay a new foundation in your mind that will support the new programs that can eradicate anxiety and depression from your life. Albert Einstein once said, "We cannot solve our problems with the same thinking we used when we created them." Applying the philosophies I teach in this book will allow you to transform your life from pain and suffering to peace and power. In

Part III, you will learn the tools and techniques I teach and use to help people successfully reprogram their subconscious minds and take back control of their lives. Once you learn these tools and techniques, and become fluent with them, you will experience powerful growth and transformation in your life.

First let's take a moment to make sure this book is for you. It's important to be up front and honest with you so that I can best assist you in overcoming anxiety and depression. The essential ingredients in overcoming any challenge, conquering any goal, or creating any real, lasting change in your life are self-discipline, patience, and practice. If you are serious about creating change in your life, you must be consistent with the implementation of these tools, disciplined in your practice, and patient throughout your process of growth. There is no magic pill or cure. It takes work, but I can tell you that now that I'm on the other side of the work, I would do it ten times over again. The process is simple, but it's not necessarily easy. I often say that change is easy. It's the most natural thing in life. It happens automatically, without any input or interference from us. The difficulty we experience when trying to change is letting go of the things that keep us from the change we desire. We tend to hold on to things in life, even those things that don't serve us well. I call these anchors, and they keep us stuck. It will take implementation and consistency if you want to create and sustain the results long term.

I believe you have chosen this book for a reason. I believe that the philosophies and system I teach can help you get on your feet to begin living life the way you truly want. I believe this book can send you well on your way to freedom, happiness, and peace. I have watched countless clients who have suffered all their lives, who have never experienced true happiness, and those who have been through trauma and heartache get back on their feet, take control of their lives in just a matter of a few months, and live their lives completely free from debilitating anxiety and depression. It doesn't take an extreme amount of time if you utilize the tools and techniques consistently, but it's all up to you to implement them. It's up to you to do the work. What you put into it, you will get out of it. I tell you this because it's the truth and is what you must first understand if you truly want to change your experience.

Take a journey with me as I share my philosophies and teach you how I have helped so many people finally live great lives free from debilitating anxiety and depression.

# PART I

# UNDERSTANDING THE MIND

# CHAPTER 1

# MEASURING AND TRACKING ANXIETY AND DEPRESSION

Anxiety and depression can wreak havoc on your personal, professional, and social life if it goes untreated for an extended time. Many people try their best to ignore the symptoms, thinking they will get better after a specific situation is over or when they finally get out of a particular circumstance that has triggered them into feelings or reactions of anxiety or depression. By the time most people seek help for these problems, it's often out of their control and has taken over their lives. Once this happens, the battle can become fierce and often very painful for them and all who are involved in their life. This downward spiral can lead to despair and a distorted perception of reality that entails hopelessness and helplessness for the individual.

Over the past few decades, we have made great strides in understanding more about what anxiety and depression are as well as the difference between the two. However, much of our learnings and understandings have not become common knowledge amongst the general population. In modern society, when people feel anxious for extended periods or experience a panic attack followed by pain or pressure in the chest, they believe they are suffering from anxiety. When people experience sadness for an extended period or they are going through a mental low in their life where they cry excessively, they believe they have depression, which is usually followed by a visit to their primary care doctor or physician, where they are prescribed some form of antianxiety or antidepressant medication to help them cope. Sometimes medications can be of great assistance in managing anxiety or depression brought on by temporary external situations such as when facing the loss of a loved one or dealing with a significant sickness that interrupts the normal flow of life. But what about long-term anxiety and depression? Or when you find yourself in repeated cycles that diminish the quality of your life? What about when anxiety and depression are commonplace in your everyday existence?

Though I don't work with medications directly, I do believe that everything has value to some degree, depending on the situation and how it is applied. Many years ago, I was prescribed Effexor XR to help me through a time of grief. Another time, when I was going through a major depression, I was prescribed Celexa. (This was before I began to live based on the philosophies in this book and understand how to work with the subconscious mind to overcome anxiety and depression.) However, I only took them long enough to help me get back on my feet so I could move forward in my life. The purpose of medication is only to help you get back on your feet when you've been knocked down by life in a major way. That's it. Unfortunately, many people end up taking them for years and even decades to try to live normal, healthy lives. They become dependent on these medications, which end up creating addictions, codependency, and even more anxiety or depression in the end. It does not have to be this way. Over the course of the following chapters, I will teach you my philosophies as well as how to utilize the subconscious mind to help you achieve a life free from debilitating anxiety and depression. In addition, you will learn to effectively manage these conditions as well as improve the quality of your life in the very same way I achieved it and have helped many others achieve it.

Whether you suffer from one of the many forms of anxiety such as general anxiety, social anxiety, agoraphobia, or even OCD, you *can* live a normal, healthy life. The same applies to depression. I repeatedly watch people become free from these debilitating conditions and begin living their lives with passion, purpose, peace, and freedom. Everybody gets knocked down in life and catches bad breaks here and there. That's life! It happens to all of us, some more than others. You or someone you know may be one of those who have been knocked down by life and can't seem to find their way back to solid ground long enough to get back up. I'm here to tell you that you can and it's time to get back up. When working on these issues in the conscious and subconscious mind, incorporating these philosophies, and utilizing specific psychological tools, the result of relief can be permanent and often much faster than medications. Moreover, there is an additional bonus of no adverse side effects—not something you hear often these days, huh?

A certain level of anxiety and depression are normal conditions that everybody experiences from time to time. But that's not the anxiety and depression I'm discussing in this book. I'm speaking to those of you who experience anxiety or depression regularly. Those of you who have just about lost all hope or are tired of being on the prescription merry-go-round. Those of you who are unhappy in life as it is and believe you are all out of options. And those of you who have become everything you never wanted to be and want nothing more than to get back to that vibrant person who was once so passionate about life that you know is hidden somewhere deep within you, just waiting to break free. I'm speaking directly to you, the one who has picked up this book with hopes of finding something that finally works. Nevertheless, there is one stipulation: you must be ready to let go of the things that are causing you pain and step into a new way of thinking and being. Surprisingly, many people are not yet willing to let go of the things that are making them sick in order to become well. Every behavior and feeling has a purpose and a payoff.

As you begin working on overcoming anxiety or depression in your life, it is essential to know if what you are or have been experiencing in your life is anxiety or depression and to what degree you are suffering. I use the Burns Anxiety Inventory and the Burns Depression Checklist to measure what level of depression and anxiety my clients experience, which helps me to understand what level of treatment is necessary for them as well as keep track of their progress as we work together. Take a few moments to go through the following two questionnaires to measure your levels of anxiety and depression. These scales should give you an accurate reflection of the levels you currently experience in your life. As you work through this book and implement these teachings and tools, use these assessments weekly to help you track your progress.

## Burns Anxiety Inventory

Directions: Select the number that best describes how much each symptom or problem has bothered or affected you based on how you have felt over the past week, including today.

0 = Not at all 1 = Somewhat 2 = Moderately 3 = A lot

1. Anxiety, nervousness, worry, or fear
2. Feeling that things around you are strange, unreal, or foggy
3. Feeling detached from all or part of your body
4. Sudden unexpected panic spells
5. Apprehension or sense of impending doom
6. Feeling tense, stressed, uptight, or on edge
7. Difficulty concentrating
8. Racing thoughts or having your mind jump from one thing to the next
9. Frightening fantasies or daydreams
10. Feeling that you're on the verge of losing control
11. Fears of cracking up or going crazy
12. Fears of fainting or passing out
13. Fears of physical illnesses or heart attacks or dying
14. Concerns about looking foolish or inadequate in front of others
15. Fears of being alone, isolated, or abandoned
16. Fears of criticism or disapproval
17. Fears that something terrible is about to happen
18. Skipping, racing, or pounding of the heart (sometimes called palpitations)
19. Pain, pressure, or tightness in the chest
20. Tingling or numbness in the toes or fingers
21. Butterflies or discomfort in the stomach
22. Constipation or diarrhea

23. Restlessness or jumpiness
24. Tight, tense muscles
25. Sweating not brought on by heat
26. A lump in the throat
27. Trembling or shaking
28. Rubbery or "jelly" legs
29. Feeling dizzy, lightheaded, or off-balance
30. Choking or smothering sensations or difficulty breathing
31. Headaches or pains in the neck or back
32. Hot flashes or cold chills
33. Feeling tired, weak, or easily exhausted

Score Results: _____

0–4 = Minimal or no anxiety

5–10 = Borderline anxiety

11–20 = Mild anxiety

21–30 = Moderate anxiety

31–50 = Severe anxiety

51–99 = Extreme anxiety or panic

## Burns Depression Checklist

Directions: Select the number that best describes how much each symptom or problem has bothered or affected you based on how you have felt over the past week, including today.

0 = Not at all 1 = Somewhat 2 = Moderately 3 = A lot 4 = Extremely

1. Feeling sad or down in the dumps
2. Feeling unhappy or blue

3. Crying spells or tearfulness
4. Feeling discouraged
5. Feeling hopeless
6. Low self-esteem
7. Feeling worthless or inadequate
8. Guilt or shame
9. Criticizing yourself or blaming others
10. Difficulty making decisions
11. Loss of interest in family, friends, or colleagues
12. Loneliness
13. Spending less time with family or friends
14. Loss of motivation
15. Loss of interest in work or other activities
16. Avoiding work or other activities
17. Loss of pleasure or satisfaction in life
18. Feeling tired
19. Difficulty sleeping or sleeping too much
20. Decreased or increased appetite
21. Loss of interest in sex
22. Worrying about your health
23. Do you have any suicidal thoughts?
24. Would you like to end your life?
25. Do you have a plan for harming yourself?

Score Results: _____

0–5 = No depression

6–10 = Normal but unhappy

11–25 = Mild depression

26–50 = Moderate depression

51–75 = Severe depression

76–100 = Extreme depression

# CHAPTER 2

# THE THEORY OF MIND

The subconscious mind is undoubtedly a fascinating topic in psychology and, as of late, in the field of quantum physics. We understand many things about how the subconscious mind works, but there is still so much to learn. I would be a fool to say I fully understand every aspect of the subconscious mind, but I will try to help you understand the things that I have come to learn about how it works. I believe that to utilize a tool to its fullest potential, I must first be able to understand it and the concepts behind it. It must be tangible and logical in a way that allows me to work with it effectively. I've done my best to create a logical explanation to explain something that is far from common logic. It is equally important to know about and understand the conscious mind as well to overcome anxiety and depression because it holds great power to influence change in the subconscious mind and is often the leading cause of self-sabotage.

## Theory of Mind

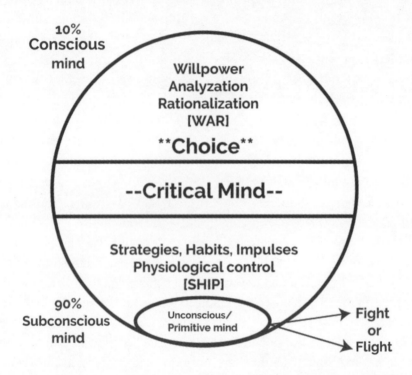

10%
Conscious
mind

Willpower
Analyzation
Rationalization
[WAR]

**Choice**

--Critical Mind--

Strategies, Habits, Impulses
Physiological control
[SHIP]

90%
Subconscious
mind

Unconscious/
Primitive mind

→ Fight
or
→ Flight

## The Conscious and Subconscious Mind

The conscious mind makes up between 5 and 10 percent of our minds and is where we become aware of things through our senses. It is responsible for willpower, which is your ability to "force" yourself to do or not to do something; analyzation, which is your process of reasoning and understanding; rationalization, which is how you break things down in manageable ways that help you justify your actions and perceptions; and most importantly, choice. Most people try to create change in their lives through the conscious mind but typically find themselves struggling or failing to create long-term results. Though the conscious mind is not where change occurs, it is essential to learn an effective way to process the information coming through it to support the new subconscious programs you desire to install. The conscious mind is the state of awareness, and when we have an awareness of something, we gain the ability to make choices concerning it. The more aware we are, the more options we have. The philosophies and teachings in this book will help you learn how to use your conscious mind to create change in your subconscious mind. Since the conscious mind is the first point of entry for external stimulus or information, it is imperative to prime and recondition it in a more effective way that will produce more effective results in your life. Most people have learned that the information that comes through their senses from the external world is or happens precisely as it appears and feels. This is rarely true. Through the teachings in this book, you will learn a much higher level of thinking that will reshape your entire existence.

The subconscious mind is where all things come together to form your experiences. It's where all your strategies, habits, impulses, physiological control, thoughts, imagination, and associations are created and reside. In other words, it's everything that makes you who you are and dictates why you do what you do in life. The subconscious mind contains all the associations you have gathered and learned throughout your entire life. All your belief systems and programs are stored there, which creates your perceptions of reality. I like to use the metaphor of a laptop computer as an example to explain the mind in a way that gives a good overview and understanding of how each part works. Think of the housing and cover as the body and the hard drive as the brain. The software on the hard drive would be considered the subconscious mind. The software dictates how information is processed and creates associations, or "links," between different information based on the way the program is designed to function.

The computer screen shows the results of the software in the form of pictures and words. Think of these as ideas and thoughts presented to the conscious mind. When we look out into the world, what we see is only a result of subconscious programming. You are unaware of 99 percent of the subconscious programs running in the background, and it would be impossible to understand or even process that much information through the conscious mind. It would be like looking at all the software code behind what you see on your computer screen. It is essential to understand that anytime a change happens within your beliefs, perceptions, opinions, or ideas that affects your thought processes and experiences, it occurs in the subconscious code. It's as if the program has been altered or rewritten in some way. Like a laptop computer's software, the subconscious mind has one primary job: to run the programs installed the way they are designed to run. It is not a logical creature and cannot decipher between good and bad or right and wrong. It merely does what it is taught to do: run a set of programs. This can be good or bad news, depending on the programs it is running. Your subconscious mind is designed to run your programs flawlessly, even if they are flawed programs. If you want to change your experiences in life, you must teach and recondition your subconscious mind to run a new program that creates the new experiences you wish to have. There are a few steps to understanding how to achieve rewriting the programs, beginning with awareness.

Awareness is known as the key to life. We can change that which we are aware of. We have little to no direct control over that which we are unaware of, and rarely can we change it, at least intentionally. In traditional therapy, mindfulness is a tool often used to bring about an awareness of one's thoughts, actions, and results. I utilize this great tool in specific, strategic ways when working with people because it can be very effective. An example of this with someone trying to overcome anxiety would be to observe the thought patterns during periods of anxiety. This observation can sometimes lead to understanding your thought patterns, giving you an ability to change your focus at the moment or understand more deeply what types of thought patterns bring on the feelings and experiences of anxiety so you can address and overcome them. Understanding and implementing awareness into your life can have a significant impact on your experiences, and I highly encourage becoming a "witness" to your thought processes as often as possible to learn more about your subconscious programming. To do this, begin to pay attention to your thoughts at any given time. Observe them with an unattached, curious mind. You will begin to learn and understand your patterns and thought processes driving the actions you take. In part II, you will learn practical ways of achieving this with great effectiveness.

## The Language of the Subconscious Mind

Let's do a simple experiment. Take about one or two minutes to close your eyes and think about yourself and your life the way you would like it to be, as if you have achieved the level of success or relief you would most love to experience. Take notice of what's going on in your mind. What happened? Did you see anything? Hear anything? Feel anything? Did you get an idea of what that might be like? That is the language of the subconscious mind. It interprets everything through pictures and stories. As simple as this may be, many people find difficulty in simplicity. We sometimes like to complicate or overthink things we haven't learned about or don't fully understand. But the truth is, to change the subconscious mind, we must change the stories within it. Think of it as a movie reel that plays the same story repeatedly. This is your program, and to change the program, you must change the story. This means we must send new pictures and stories to the subconscious mind.

This is where hypnotherapy and other subconscious tools, such as neurolinguistic programming (NLP), make a huge difference. With these tools, we can bypass the conscious mind and implant the new story and pictures directly in the subconscious mind where the programming exists. This is simple, but it's not easy. It takes self-discipline, patience, practice, and a willingness to implement changes in your life. Even using hypnotherapy, which some believe to be a magic pill that will cure them instantly, there must be a will to change and the self-discipline to put into action new techniques and systems. There must be congruency between the conscious and subconscious mind if you want to change your experiences.

Reprogramming the subconscious mind to change the experiences you have in life is a matter of changing the stories within it of who you are and your relationship with the world. It's important to give a little more detail of what a story in the subconscious mind is, or instead, what it consists of. Your story comes from your beliefs about yourself, who you are, what you are, the world, and everything you have ever encountered. It's your identification, even if it's a story of not knowing who you are or one that creates feelings of confusion and displacement about yourself or the world around you. How you interact with the world stems from the perceptions created by your belief systems. Your belief systems come from previous learnings and experiences that you have gained throughout your life from your caretakers, friends, influences, and environment. Most people believe that events create experiences. This is not the case. If it were, everyone would have the same experience with an event. Events are neutral. They have no negative or positive value until you decide their value. Events trigger internal representations (associations and relationships to events), which come from the belief systems you hold. It is your internal representation or association with the event that creates your experience with it.

## Event + Internal Representation = Experience

### (Associations/relationship to an event)

Creating a new experience does not necessarily depend on creating a new event, environment, or external circumstances. Your experiences are not created by the events that take place outside of you but instead through a process of identification based on what you have learned about the events, circumstances, or conditions. They are catalysts that stimulate associations within your subconscious mind. The associations create a chemical response in the brain that forms a thought pattern. The thought pattern then creates an emotional response in the body, leading to a preconditioned action or behavior. This, in turn, creates your results. Here is the formula:

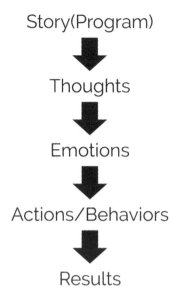

Story(Program)

⬇

Thoughts

⬇

Emotions

⬇

Actions/Behaviors

⬇

Results

This process creates the results and experiences in our lives. In most cases, when people don't like the results in their lives, they seek new behaviors. They take new actions to create different outcomes so they can have new experiences in life. While this sounds good and is the most common approach to life, it's not a very effective strategy for long-term success. If it were, you probably wouldn't be reading this book right now. To create different results, you must understand what created them to begin with. The stories or programs within the subconscious mind are the causes, while the results are the effects.

When people seek out new behaviors as a way of creating change in their lives, they are only working with the last part of the process that created them. This is typically ineffective for sustaining the change they desire. We can see this in many aspects of others' lives where they have taken different actions or changed their behaviors to produce new results but continue to recreate similar situations and conditions. Imagine if you could see your life with the same level of objectivity and observation as you can someone else's. You may see how you do the same thing in various parts of your life as well. How many ways have you approached the cycles of anxiety or depression in your life just to end up where you began? While it is necessary to change the actions, by only engaging in this part of the process, you are far less likely to reach the core factors in the subconscious mind to change what's propelling them. It's not an effective approach to produce real change and long-term results in life. The most effective way to create the change you desire in life is by changing the cause of your results, the subconscious programs. That's what this book is designed to help you achieve—change in the subconscious mind—so you can produce and create long-term results in your life that are sustainable and effective.

## The Critical Mind

The critical mind is the filtration system that separates the conscious from the subconscious mind. Its job is to filter out the things that "don't belong," those things that would interrupt or disrupt the current program, story, or ideas that don't resonate with the prevailing belief systems in the subconscious mind. The critical mind is developed between the ages of eight and twelve and serves as a guide to help you make decisions and "protect" yourself from harmful input. When information or stimulus is received from the external world in the conscious mind, before it goes into the subconscious mind, it must pass through this filter. Information will remain in the critical mind to be sorted out for approximately thirty-five to forty minutes. If it does not resonate, or "belong," as part of your subconscious programming, it will be released. This system is beneficial and can prevent a lot of harmful and unwanted programming from coming in and taking over. For example, if someone you are talking to tries to convince you that robbing a bank is okay and justified, without this filtration system in place, they could more easily persuade you of their belief. Of course, this an extreme example, but it shows how beneficial the critical mind is.

Though the critical mind can be very beneficial when it comes to unwanted input becoming part of the subconscious programming, it can also make installing wanted and desired information difficult. The subconscious mind is a creature of habit, and it doesn't like change. For this reason, installing a new program or tweaking an old one can be a bit tricky and, at times, very difficult. You can move information past this filtration system in many ways, but it doesn't come without a cost. Some of the more common methods of trying to achieve this are affirmations, repetition of a new habit, or hiring an accountability partner to help you stay on track with new behaviors. These can be beneficial and helpful ways to achieve this goal; however, they can take a lot of energy and time to work on their own. Most people don't have the patience or self-discipline to carry out a daily practice for the length of time it takes to convince the subconscious mind to accept the new programming with these methods.

Change can be hard and takes a lot of work when using conscious tools to push new programs past the critical mind. Therefore, I work systematically with my clients and teach them techniques to ensure their conscious efforts penetrate the subconscious barrier. To penetrate the subconscious mind using the conscious mind, you must be able to affect the belief systems in place by directly exposing their weaknesses and implanting a replacement that satisfies whatever part or aspect of yourself it is designed to preserve or protect. I will teach you how to do this in the upcoming chapters of this book.

## The Primitive Mind

The primitive mind refers to the most fundamental part of the mind that deals with fight or flight. These are our basic survival instincts designed to keep us out of danger and preserve our lives. One of the challenges people who suffer from anxiety and depression experience is turning their primitive minds on and off when necessary. For example, when anxiety hits and you're in public, your flight mode may kick in and push you to run away from the perceived threat of the situation. Though it is designed to keep you safe, it doesn't always achieve that goal because, just like the subconscious mind, it cannot dictate right from wrong or good from bad. It runs based on the programs in the subconscious mind. If earlier in life you encountered a traumatic situation while in the middle of a crowd and your subconscious mind learned to associate crowds with danger or trauma, you will find those defense mechanisms kicking in and the flight mode engaged to move you away from a crowd to safety. When working to relieve anxiety and depression, this is one of the programs you must change. Again, this is not a bad thing. As in the example above, the primitive mind is designed to keep you safe and preserve your life.

## Right versus Left Brain

Both hemispheres of the brain are necessary to understand when working to overcome the challenges of anxiety and depression. Each has its strengths and weaknesses, but the most effective way to get relief from and overcome these conditions is to utilize both hemispheres. The left region of the brain is known as the logical side of the brain. It is good with math, science, and things that require a certain amount of calculation and logic to understand. When working on yourself, it is essential to satisfy this side of the brain with specifics that are down to earth, tangible, and understandable from a logistics point of view by using real-world knowledge and comprehensible language to describe and understand the challenges and a path to a solution. When you set goals for yourself as you work toward healing and overcoming anxiety and depression, the steps you focus on must be logical, intellectually understood, and comprehensible to satisfy this side of the brain. Therefore, you need to know what you're experiencing and how the mind works. It's why knowledge is necessary for your journey to recovery and freedom.

For example, understanding the subconscious mind as a system that produces a specific response in a situation can help you intellectually know what's happening as you go through it and help you create a solution or plan to counteract those responses when they arise. When you understand this and can identify it from a logical standpoint, you have satisfied the left side of the brain. The primary way I help my clients satisfy the left side of the brain is through a systematic structure that allows them to break their experiences down into manageable steps to understand the effects and purpose of each response they experience.

For many years, I have strived to make sense of the subconscious mind and processes we go through in a way that makes it clear and understandable to just about anyone. I believe this to be necessary when helping someone achieve relief from anxiety and depression—or any goal, for that matter.

The right hemisphere of the brain is most known for creativity and imagination. It's believed to be the most powerful when implementing change, and I agree. One of the reasons for this is that the subconscious mind cannot tell the difference between what's real or imagined. A great example of this is to reflect on a time when you watched a sad movie that made you feel very emotional or even cry. What you saw was only a story played out by actors and actresses in a controlled environment for entertainment purposes. It wasn't real, but that didn't stop your subconscious mind from believing and reacting to it as if it were. Whatever you think, no matter what it is you are thinking of, you always think in pictures and stories. Sound familiar? Of course, it's the language of the subconscious mind. This is the primary hemisphere responsible for your creative thoughts, while the left hemisphere is responsible for understanding those thoughts in a way that makes sense and that you can work with logically to apply in your life. Utilizing this hemisphere is the key to unlocking the door to your subconscious mind.

For many years, sports psychologists and peak performance coaches have used visualization with their clients who are professional sports players. Some prominent names you may be familiar with who have used this to gain elite status and break records are Tiger Woods and Mike Tyson. They began using visualization and hypnosis to create specific stories and outcomes in their minds at a very young age, which helped lead them to great success in the sports world. This technique has shown significant improvements in performance and results for many. Some people claim not to be good at visualizing or using their imaginations. However, with practice, this skill can be learned and refined. For example, think about what the inside of your bedroom looks like. Notice all the colors and designs. Look around and see all the furniture in the room. Were you able to see the inside of your room successfully? Most likely. The more you practice, the better you will get. It's like a muscle that will grow in strength each time you work it out.

Since the left hemisphere of the brain likes to dissect and break things down analytically, you must be careful not to allow your intellect to sabotage your potential. Since the left strives for logical or mathematical understanding, it can sometimes get in the way of progress or healing because often we are not sure of what to do or how things will work out. You may visualize yourself living a different life with the right hemisphere, but the left may quickly object with logic or reasoning based on what it knows and has learned from the past. It may tell you that it's impossible to achieve those goals or ideas because it can't figure out exactly how it will take form or unfold in your life. You must learn to exercise control over these types of thoughts. I will teach you processes to address these, as well as the issue of control, in the upcoming chapters.

## Neural Pathways

Many people associate change with different results or experiences in their lives, but it's essential to understand that change happens on a biological level as well. Change occurs within the brain through the formation of new neural pathways. Each thought is a product of a connection between two nerve cells taking place in the brain; this is called synapsis. When a stimulus comes in through the senses, it creates an electrical discharge that connects one nerve cell to another. This connection produces a chemical response that creates thought patterns based on what the subconscious mind is familiar with through past learnings and belief systems.

When we sustain a new response through efforts or tools designed to change the automatic or programmed response for long enough, a new neural pathway forms in the brain, producing a new automatic response. This process typically takes thirteen or more weeks of consistency and is why many programs such as drug rehabs are ninety-day programs. Once these new neural pathways have formed, your new responses become automatic. This doesn't mean you're done with all the work. The old pathways are still there waiting for the opportunity to be used again. Therefore, you must have structures in place that continue to keep you on the path of growth. I like to think about this as a diamond. It has many facets, and sometimes, when we believe we've fleshed out all the details of a problem or program, there may still be a facet we have not yet become aware of. That is why this book addresses the philosophies and belief patterns in a way to change them permanently so that when this happens, you will have the tools you need to address them successfully.

## How the Subconscious Mind Learns

The subconscious mind learns and forms programs in two primary ways: repetition and highly charged emotional experiences. If you look back on your life, you will notice that most things you remember are either things that you did repetitively or things that had a high emotional charge. High emotionally charged experiences that are negative, such as trauma, are the reason many people get stuck reliving the experiences of the events and develop what's known as post-traumatic stress disorder (PTSD). This happens with a lot with people who have lost someone they love, have been abused, or military personnel who have been to war.

We are taught from a young age in school to review and study material over and over to learn it because repetition is a critical factor for installing a program as well. Therefore, consistency and focus are essential when creating change in your life. It's also why many people repeat affirmations or use visualization with feeling or emotion. A process in the brain called the reticular activating system (RAS) drives information with high emotional responses into the mind quickly. This process filters out unimportant information and pushes in new information that can influence your belief systems. By sending highly charged emotions connected to thoughts or experiences into your mind, you activate this system and create change much faster and more effectively. This is useful to know, especially when it comes to anxiety and depression, for both send strong emotional signals to the brain, which works to keep you in the cycles. When you experience anxiety and depression for long periods, which typically consist of high emotional charges, the compounding effects can be devastating. We will use both learning formats throughout this book to help you impose the most effective change possible to your subconscious mind.

# CHAPTER 3

# SYMPTOMS VERSUS PROBLEMS

Anxiety and depression are common terms in our society today. Most people either have had a personal experience with these conditions or know someone who has. For some who experience anxiety, this annoying nervousness seems to linger in certain situations or around specific events, while others may experience panic attacks and a complete loss of control of their thoughts and emotions, which paralyzes them. For those who experience depression, the symptoms can range from feeling a deep sadness on a regular or extended basis to experiencing suicidal thoughts and ideations. While the range of symptoms can vary from person to person, there are some common symptoms experienced by most people with these conditions. However, what anxiety and depression are is widely misunderstood by the general population as well as by many in the field of psychology and medicine.

To overcome anxiety and depression, you must understand what they are and why they are there. I'm not referring to the events that created them or what took place to begin the cycles. I am referring to what is taking place that causes these conditions to continue in the present. It may sound surprising, but anxiety and depression are not problems; they are symptoms. They can be extremely problematic in your life because they create unwanted or harmful experiences, but they are symptoms. They are the result of the conflict in the subconscious programs. It's not always easy to identify exactly where the anxiety or depression began, but overcoming these conditions does not require knowing exactly where they came from or what first created the conflict. It's essential to understand the difference between problems and symptoms. Symptoms are an indicator of problems. If we didn't have them, we wouldn't know there was a conflict that needed resolving. Many medications and anxiety/depression treatment programs don't typically work well for people because they are only addressing the symptoms rather than the problems that created them. These symptoms have a purpose that is useful—but only when we understand how to use them.

## Defense Mechanisms

Defense mechanisms play a vital role in your subconscious mind, and they can be seen in many, if not all, parts of your life. Though it may not seem logical as it applies to anxiety and depression from a conscious viewpoint, defense mechanisms are there to help you. Their job is to keep you within your comfort zone and safe from uncertain situations that could cause you harm. It's one of the ways your mind maintains your survival. Let's look at how this can apply to anxiety.

A former client of mine experienced social anxiety and would begin to feel a sense of panic when surrounded by crowds of people during ball games, in the mall, or at the grocery store. His mind and heart would begin to race, and it was only a short time before he would make a beeline to the door to escape the situation. He was forty-two years old when he came to see me and explained that he had been experiencing anxiety since he was around twelve or thirteen years old. He talked about how he suffered a humiliating episode where he did something very embarrassing at school one day while in front of many of his classmates. This experience had a high emotional charge for him and created a change that would soon present itself as anxiety. Since that day, he tried to avoid crowds and became insecure about himself when others were around. He didn't understand why he was like this, and his thoughts began to criticize and devalue him. This also led to a battle with depression because of what and how he thought he should be versus how he was and was being, which turned into a negative cycle that fed on itself repeatedly.

Let's examine this situation for a moment to uncover how the defense mechanism of anxiety is trying to help keep him safe. When a high emotionally charged experience of humiliation and embarrassment took place, his subconscious mind formed an association of shame and embarrassment within crowds. Since we understand that the subconscious mind only runs programs based on belief systems that are installed through what we learn and can't logically decipher things, we can determine that the anxiety that he developed was a defense mechanism designed to keep him from going out into crowds for fear of humiliation and embarrassment. This defense mechanism was very effective in keeping him away from crowds. Just knowing he would become anxious and possibly experience a panic attack or discomfort was enough to deter him from putting himself in those situations. This formed deep insecurities and negative self-talk. He began to believe that he was broken and that something was wrong with him. Finding out after almost thirty years that nothing was "wrong" with him and that his mind was working quite well came as a huge relief. We began to work on the subconscious relationships and associations with crowds to install new ones based on a belief that they were now safe for him to be in or around. He is now part of a local community club where he is involved in many fundraising activities in public, and he doesn't have any issues going out to public places or being around crowds anymore.

I mentioned previously that defense mechanisms are there to help a person. This applies to depression as well. Depression is often accompanied by a deep sadness, regrets, or guilt that lingers. It steals passion and purpose from a person and leaves them feeling stuck, worthless, and hopeless. A former client of mine came to see me after she had been depressed for several years, to the point where she couldn't even bring herself to get out of bed most days. She lost all desire and passion for living and felt stuck and powerless over her thoughts and experiences. She talked about how she suffered through many traumas and was mistreated throughout her life.

As if her experience of depression weren't enough, she developed anxiety at the mere thought of having to get out of bed and be around others. Her life became a battle with both anxiety and depression. Through many tears and pouring out her heart and soul just for one glimmer of hope that things could turn around for her, I helped her begin to understand how the defense mechanisms worked to keep her where she was. She learned that she was applying her past to her present and future, which prevented her from making more mistakes and continuing to do the wrong things. After healing and changing those associations and relationships from the past, she began to live her life free from all the baggage of the past and stepped into a life of personal power and freedom.

Let's examine her situation and how the defense mechanisms came into play to keep her in depression. When she was young, she went through some severe traumas that created negative associations and beliefs within her subconscious mind about who she was, her value, worth, and character, followed by being mistreated throughout her life. Though it was painful, her defense mechanisms wouldn't allow her to experience anything far outside of the negative associations and beliefs that had been installed so profoundly through the traumatic events due to uncertainty. Her fears of reliving the past traumas and pain caused her defense mechanisms of anxiety and depression to kick in, which were designed to keep her safe and out of harm's way. Allowing her to become something that didn't resonate or fit within the construct of her existing system could be dangerous and was therefore avoided.

Once we revealed the identification issue of who she was due to the trauma and mistreatment, we could then work to create a new identity that allowed her to interact with the world and her environment in a way that changed her experience into one of passion, purpose, happiness, and motivation. She was a wife and a mother of a teenage boy. When she healed these parts of herself, she was able to form and sustain healthy relationships and be a positive influence for her husband and son.

## Pain versus Pleasure Principle

Now that you understand more clearly what anxiety and depression are, as well as how the mind uses them to help you, it's essential to understand the purpose of pain. Anxiety and depression are forms of pain and distress within the mind and the body. Pain is viewed by most as a negative thing that causes bad experiences. While I agree that pain is uncomfortable and can be very debilitating in many ways, I also understand that pain is necessary and useful as well. I often say that it's one of our greatest assets in life because it is our most powerful motivator. When you face enough pain, you are likely to move or attempt to move away from whatever is causing you pain and get yourself into a more pleasurable state.

The pain versus pleasure principle governs almost every aspect of our lives. This principle states that we are always looking to move away from pain and into higher levels of pleasure. Sigmund Freud believed this to be the driving force of the ego and that our entire life revolves around it. Some people ask, "If this is true, then why am I stuck in pain and unable to move into a more pleasurable state?" It's a fair question. The answer, however, is not cut-and-dried and can vary depending on the situation and circumstances, but I will do my best to help you understand how and why this happens. It's useful to note that the pain associated with anxiety is often more pleasurable than the pain associated with the fear of the unknown. This can have a significant impact on where you are as well as the level of pain you are experiencing.

Let's recap for a moment what we've learned about the subconscious mind to understand what is happening to keep you in the painful state of anxiety and depression. The subconscious mind is not a logical creature. It simply runs programs based on past learnings and experiences. These programs do not change as you evolve and grow older unless new programs are installed to replace them. It has strict boundaries based around the things it has learned. When you move close to those boundaries, you risk stepping into the unknown. The unknown creates fear and destabilization in the subconscious mind, which causes your defense mechanisms to kick in, bringing you back into your comfort zone.

Again, the subconscious mind is a creature of habit and is extremely uncomfortable with change. As illustrated in the previous example of my former client who experienced social anxiety, going into a crowd was out of his comfort zone. Anytime he thought about or went into a crowd, his defense mechanisms would kick in by creating an experience of anxiety to protect him from the danger that may exist in those circumstances. Then it created an experience of depression based on his idea of what *should be* versus what *was* at that time in his life. It was the difference in his mind of where he was and where he thought he should be that created the experience of depression, which only worsened his experience of anxiety. This happens anytime you breach or come close to moving out of your comfort zone. Your comfort zone is created throughout your life by the things you have learned from your caregivers, peers, environment, and even your personal internal experiences and discoveries. Defense mechanisms form what we refer to as symptoms designed to help and protect you, so they will kick in as an indicator that you are moving into an unknown or uncertainty to bring you back to your comfort zone of familiarity.

Pain is necessary because it lets us know that there is a problem. Imagine spraining your ankle. What would you experience? Pain. You don't experience the sprain of the ankle directly but instead the response from the nerves in the form of pain as a communication to the brain that there is something wrong. If there were no pain, you would continue trying to walk on it, which could cause more damage to the ankle. Once the problem is corrected and the ankle heals, what happens to the pain? It disappears. Pain has a purpose and is necessary. You may say that you don't like pain or that it's not good but understanding the purpose it serves will give you a greater respect for it.

The great thing about physical pain is that it can help us identify exactly where and (most times) what the problem is. Emotional pain is different because we don't always know where or what the problem is to correct it. However, we do know that it comes from the mental state and that we can change or adjust it to relieve the pain. Don't be afraid of this pain. It's there to help you by revealing there is a conflict. The proper thing to do to relieve this pain is to address the conflict causing it. This is where many people get stuck. They focus on the pain as if it is the problem, which then creates more problems. They do everything they can to get relief from the pain, which means they are only addressing the symptoms of pain, not the actual problem. This is important. If you only treat the symptoms, it will recur or, even worse, become debilitating.

Do not fear the pain you go through in life. Begin to use pain for the purpose it is meant to serve—to help you become aware of internal conflict so you can resolve it. When the problem is resolved, the pain will serve no purpose and dissolve. Pain doesn't just happen, and it is not a bad thing. It may feel bad, but don't let your feelings and emotional pain define you; let them refine you. You will learn how to achieve this in the upcoming chapters.

When you resolve the problems and the pain subsides, you will have greater levels of peace and freedom in your life. This doesn't mean to avoid addressing the pain; just don't get stuck in it. Sometimes it is useful and even necessary to reduce the pain to work on the problem because pain can have a way of creating more problems or dysfunctions in life that may distract you from the cause of it. This is where medication for anxiety or depression has been beneficial for many people. The downside is that when the pain subsides whether entirely or significantly, many people don't return to address the problem that created it so they're stuck on medications for long periods or fight a continuous battle with anxiety and depression. If you want real peace and freedom in your life, you must resolve these underlying issues, not just address the pain they cause.

## The Fear Factor

Fear is anxiety and depression's best friend and is the catalyst to these conditions. Fear is the result of uncertainty. When you're uncertain about something, there can be a follow-up of worry, doubt, and fear. This doesn't apply to everything in your life, only the things that have made or have the potential to make an impact in your life. This is true even for those things that you only perceive as affecting your life. For example, you may not typically experience fear if your spouse or someone you love is late getting home one evening. But what if you had just heard on the news that there was a wreck five miles from your house on the road they were driving? This would likely create a state of fear, followed by anxiety. If it were your spouse or loved one involved in that wreck and their life changed for what seemed like the worse, it could cause anxiety to follow based on the uncertainty of what's to come and depression based on the difference or comparison of what was and what is. Most of the time, this would only cause temporary anxiety or depression, but if it was traumatic enough, it could lead to long-term effects.

Let's look at the other side of this scenario. What if it were you involved in that wreck and you had a traumatic experience that left you with anxiety when you drove or rode in a car? I have worked with this common scenario many times. When a program is interrupted due to a traumatic experience, it removes the preexisting beliefs about that event and replaces them based on the new experience. The reason for this is that the subconscious mind is programmed through high emotionally charged experiences. In this case, driving becomes a dangerous and unpredictable event that can cause harm according to the new program. When the activity of driving becomes associated with uncertainty and fear, the program of psychological security and safety has become interrupted and defense mechanisms kick in that create states of anxiety or other symptoms designed to keep you from driving or riding in vehicles. This doesn't happen on the same level for everyone, for everyone relates to things differently. Some people suffer for many years, if not their entire lifetime, when something like this happens, while others may only have slight anxiety.

A typical case scenario is those people who experience anxiety regularly without a specific identifiable trigger, which can happen for several reasons. One of the most common is when people begin to feel stuck in life. This is when they feel paralyzed and unable to move forward because they are unsure of which direction to proceed. Their lives begin to revolve around fear and the inability to cope with day-to-day activities. They slowly lose the most precious things in life, such as purpose, passion, motivation, and self-value. It affects their relationships, careers, and many other things, which keeps them in a cycle of anxiety and depression. Before they know it, they're in a debilitating cycle that feeds on itself and continues to take them further down the rabbit hole. Everything becomes uncertain and fearful, which causes even more anxiety. The thought of moving forward becomes fearful, and though feeling stuck is painful, they are already there and will continue to stay there until it becomes too painful to no longer move. This is when the change will typically begin to occur. Tony Robbins once said, "Change happens when the pain of staying the same is greater than the pain of change."

Another common scenario is when anxiety is a learned response from a person's environment. An example of this is people growing up with mothers or fathers who experienced anxiety when facing difficult situations in their lives. They may learn to cope with stressful events, circumstances, or triggers in the same way. Remember, the subconscious mind is just running programs that do what they have been taught to do. How you have learned to cope with the world is something you were taught to do through your environment.

There are many reasons a person begins and continues to experience anxiety. To list them all would be nearly impossible but understanding the basic concept of where they come from and why they are there provides a foundation that can allow you to begin addressing the issues and either completely overcome or manage them with ease. Understanding defense mechanisms, how they work, and why they are there, as well as the pain versus pleasure principle, is essential when working to overcome them. No matter what level of anxiety and depression you are experiencing, no matter how long you have experienced it, and no matter who you are, you *can* overcome them. Many clients have expressed to me that they have tried "everything" and nothing seems to work for them. They feel that they are somehow immune to all the things that work for everybody else. Many traditional approaches and even medications do not work for many people. Creating the changes you are looking for requires that you resolve the conflicts in the subconscious mind that are keeping you from them. That is the solution to debilitating cycles of anxiety and depression.

# PART II

# A NEW FOUNDATION

# CHAPTER 4

# LAYING THE GROUNDWORK

As we have made great advances in the fields of psychology and science, as well as the development of new technologies that allow us to measure the effects and power of the mind, we have begun to understand more fully the impact our thought patterns and belief systems have on the situations and circumstances we experience in our lives. We have learned that they are responsible for many of the experiences we create and have in our lives. Many people try to incorporate affirmations or other daily practices such as visualization in hopes of influencing their minds to produce the things and experiences they desire. Any work that you do to change the mind to produce results that are more desirable is great, and I always encourage it. However, most people are not very effective in producing the profound effects they desire and work so hard to create. The primary reason for this is the limiting beliefs that overpower the new input.

Think about the mind as a garden. The subconscious mind would be the soil, the conscious mind would be the seeds (new ideas and programs) planted in the soil, and the products of the seeds would be the results you create in your life. The soil has one job—to grow whatever seeds are planted—and it does that job very well. It doesn't matter whether you plant roses, shrubbery, corn, or weeds. This garden has been actively growing whatever seeds have been planted in the soil from the time you were born. As a child, you were unaware of the seeds planted because you didn't understand the world and enough of how it worked to discern what was right or best for you. You were in a subconscious state for the first several years of your life and didn't have much choice over the external input. Whatever your environment expressed to you became the seeds planted in the soil.

For example, if you grew up in a situation where money was hard to come by or saw that your parents or caretakers struggled with it, the relationship or understanding that you formed with money may be that it didn't come easily or that there was a minimal supply. This became the seed planted in your soil about money. This seed grows into a weed. The reason I call this a weed is because it's not based in truth, nor does it serve you well. As an adult, you may begin to walk around saying affirmations to yourself that you are wealthy or rich and that money comes easily for you. If you do this long enough, you may rewire your brain and override that old belief system that says that money is a struggle and hard to come by. This is not the case for most people. It's like trying to throw new seeds into your soil without addressing the weeds. If you've ever tended to a garden or dealt with weeds in your yard, you know that they tend to kill all the rest of the grass or plants around them because they suck the nutrients and water from the soil. They don't just affect their immediate surroundings; they spread. Before long, your yard or flower bed becomes infested with weeds instead of beautiful grass or flowers. Without the right nutrition, the new seeds can't grow or produce to their full potential.

The approach that I have found most effective for myself and those I work with to produce new results in their lives is to address the old belief systems to remove the weeds or limiting beliefs and then plant the new seeds in their place. When we remove the old belief systems that keep the new programs from taking root and growing and then install a new belief system, it can grow and flourish. This is a process of replacement. We cannot simply delete programs; we must replace them. There can be no empty holes or spaces in the mind. The new seeds that I work with to replace the weeds are seeds of truth. In all my years of study and practice, truth is the most powerful replacement that I have ever seen or found for creating real change in life. This is a process of retraining the mind to work more effectively and efficiently.

# Mental Training

One of the most crucial understandings to know about healing and overcoming anxiety and depression is that you must become someone different or a different version of yourself that produces different results. You will still be you, just a better and more effective version of you. This will only happen through training your mind to think and act differently to help you gain a new perspective, create new thought patterns, and install new belief systems in the subconscious mind that allow you to begin living your life from a place of empowerment.

It is vitally important that you invest yourself in these tools and philosophies each day for a minimum of three months to make them permanent in your subconscious mind. This doesn't mean that it only takes three months to heal yourself. It could take a few years to fully recover from all the trauma you have experienced. Growth is like peeling layers of an onion. You must peel one layer at a time. As you grow, things will come up when they are ready to be resolved and released. This will happen automatically and without your conscious interference. When it does, you must address them. You can address them effectively by using the tools and techniques you will learn in this book. It isn't always pleasant to face these things, but it is necessary.

Anxiety and depression are results of subconscious programming. Changing the programs creating them will allow you to see and sustain new results and experiences in your life. Please don't mistake this for a motivational or "fake it till you make it" system but instead one based in science, research, and study. The way we perceive and relate to things creates our experiences with them. When we begin to work from an empowered state of mind and equip ourselves to overcome these disorders by thinking more effectively, we create powerful change that influences every aspect of our lives. Don't expect perfection or to get each step of this process right in the beginning. You may experience some struggles and difficulties with these tools and philosophies at first. Each time you become aware of yourself slipping or not implementing these tools, put them back into action immediately and pat yourself on the back for taking another step toward healing. To begin, you must accept and uphold the golden rules for creating change in your life. Honoring these rules is necessary for healing.

Rule #1: **Be good to yourself and *never* beat yourself up for your mistakes and shortcomings**

Imagine watching someone berate, belittle, and verbally criticize another person, making them feel inferior, low, and bad about themselves. What would you call that behavior? Abuse! Let me ask you a question: are you an abusive person? If the answer is yes, do you want to be an abusive person? Of course you don't. Do you deserve to be abused? Absolutely not! When you beat yourself up and put yourself down, you are both an abusive person for abusing yourself and an abused person for receiving the abuse. Is that how you want to be or live? Of course not! There is no growth in beating yourself up, period. Your mind will likely go to this place because it's a habit and something you've probably been doing to yourself for many years. Let it go. Even if you feel like those things are true about yourself, you must let them go if you want to heal. If you continue to walk around beating yourself up or putting yourself down, you will not achieve a life of freedom and happiness.

When you look at successful, happy people, you don't see them fighting themselves and rejecting who they are. They embrace their strengths and positive qualities. This is essential to your success and happiness as well. Mistakes are part of life. Their purpose is to teach you. Every mistake you have made and will make presents an opportunity for you to grow and become a stronger, better person. Mistakes are part of being human. They're part of life. It's something you cannot avoid so stop trying. Embrace them and allow them to make you better. Many people are walking around trying to be perfect. This is impossible and extremely ineffective as a strategy. Do you want to continue doing something you know isn't going to work? Of course you don't. Stop trying to be perfect and do the best you can. That's all you can do. Be okay with making mistakes and having shortcomings in your life. You have no choice—and that is perfectly okay. You may have others who hold expectations over you to be perfect. If so, let go of trying to meet their expectations. Be what you are—human. Here is an example to illustrate how you can implement this rule and begin reconditioning your mind when you become aware of beating yourself up:

**Example: I can't believe I just did that! What's wrong with me? God, I am so stupid!**

**Correction: Hold on! I'm beating myself up for a mistake again. I'm not an abusive person, and I don't deserve to be abused. I'm human, I'm going to make mistakes, and that's okay. I can learn from this. There's nothing wrong with me! I don't have to do that to myself anymore.**

Rule #2:  **Let go of your old story**

As I explained in the subconscious language section in chapter two, it's all about pictures and stories in the subconscious mind. If you want to begin living with new experiences, you must make room for them by letting go of the old ones. This doesn't mean to lie about your situation or to be fake or false in where you are but instead begin to understand that the old story is a result of your past, not your future. You can change that story, but only if you're willing to give it up for good. If you want to see something new in your life, you must become something new. I understand that you feel justified in the story you tell—this person did this, that person did that, and so on. Letting that story go doesn't let those people off the hook for the wrong they have done to you. It allows you to advance and overcome the damage and pain that it caused so that you can have a better life. It's about you, not them. Many people identify with their pasts and allow them to define who they are. You made mistakes and went through some difficult things. Maybe you have regrets about what you did, how you handled a situation, or that things didn't turn out the way you planned. That's okay. It must be okay because the truth is, that's the way it is.

It's time to come to terms with it and step into a new future that's bright, full of possibility and opportunities that will far exceed anything you have ever experienced. The only way that can happen is by letting go of your old story and making room for a new one. If your mind is always filled with the things from your past, you must empty it to have space for the new things you want to come. Otherwise, you are stuck in the experiences of your past and will never have room for new ones. It's time for new beginnings, and the great news is that you can begin right now. It's time to tell a new story about who and what you are in this world. It's your time to live a new life of freedom and happiness. Let go of your old story and begin telling a new one of healing and restoration. Here is an example to illustrate how you can implement this rule and start reconditioning your mind to tell a new story:

**Old Story: Money is a problem for me. I can never seem to get ahead.**

**New Story: My experience with money is now becoming a positive experience. I am finding new ways to increase my income and create financial freedom. I can do this!**

Rule #3:  **Do the work every day**

I wish I could tell you that you only have to do this work once or twice and you will be healed. That is not the case. If you want new and lasting results in your life, you must be diligent and consistent in this work. The subconscious mind learns through repetition. Reprogramming your mind requires you to remain as focused as possible and do this work every day. Many people ask me what the work is. It is primarily mental work but does require some physical work such as writing things down at times or making time to do the mental work. It requires that you immerse yourself in the process to yield the results. These philosophies and teachings will not spontaneously change things for you but will begin the process of changing them. You must work at them, keep them in your conscious awareness, and implement them accordingly. What I will be teaching you in this book *will* change your life magnificently and powerfully, but only if you do the work. Unfortunately, that's not negotiable. I wish it were, but it's not. Do the work even when you don't feel like it and you will see the benefits and results as you've never seen before.

You don't have to be fully on board with this promise of hope I am delivering. I am confident that if you do this work every day, you too will become a believer. Many people come to me skeptical of my claims based on their past experiences of failure to create real change in their life through self-help or professional help. This doesn't, nor has it ever, bothered me, for I know that when this work is done, it will work. It must. When you learn something new that hits the core of your being, it changes you. It's just the nature of our being. When your mind expands, it can't shrink back to what it was before. Commit every day to do the work required to implement these tools and philosophies and watch your life transform.

Rule #4: **Have an open mind**

Though some of the philosophies and tools I teach may be things you have heard before, many will also be new. Keep your mind open to trying them out. Everything I will be teaching you can be tested to see if and how it works for you. I encourage you to do so. A primary reason people don't change is that they are so rigid in their thinking. This can serve a useful purpose in some cases, but it can also hinder you from having new experiences. I like to tell people to try these things on for a few weeks, like a shirt, and see if it fits. Give it time to grow on you and see how your life changes. If you don't like it or if it doesn't fit, discard it and go about your way. Don't allow what you have learned in the past to stop you from discovering something new or different that can be beneficial. People like to continue doing the same things repeatedly while expecting different results in their life. Or they will do the same thing differently with the expectation of a new or different experience. That is an ineffective strategy and approach to changing your life, as you may have already seen.

The philosophies in this book have changed my life as well as those of many others, and I believe they can for you as well. Allow yourself to approach these teachings with a fresh, curious mind, without any preconceived notions and without any interference from what you have learned or tried in the past, without any interruption from others in the form of opinion or doubt. Be completely open to these teachings and you will see a new life awakening from within you—a life of empowerment that will lead you to freedom and happiness. It's your time to experience real results in your life, and I know that by stepping into these teachings, you too can be free from debilitating anxiety and depression—for good.

## The Impact of Your Words

The words you speak hold a lot of power, maybe more than you realize. You can heal, destroy, save, help, hurt, and much more just through the power of your words. Words are what govern companies and nations, and they are responsible for most all of the peace and war in the world. They are the catalyst that sparks these events. This area requires much attention throughout this process. The impact your words have on your life plays a big part in contributing to how it turns out. This is not about positive affirmations, ignoring negative things, or being fake but rather about understanding that the words you speak create an energetic response that can move things into motion and create a significant impact on you and your life.

Maybe you've heard the phrase "self-fulfilling prophecy." This is a very real thing that happens when someone repeats the same thing over and over to themselves and others, which then becomes part of their belief system and foundational settings. Remember, the subconscious mind learns through repetition. Once this happens, this person begins to experience whatever they continue to repeat and believe. Therefore, it's important to follow Rule #2 and speak about yourself and your life from a place of personal power and love. In the upcoming chapters, I will teach you a process that will help you speak from a place of personal power and love, but you can begin now by taking responsibility and being mindful of the words you speak and no longer allowing yourself to talk negatively about yourself or your life.

Some things will not turn out the way you want them to. Things aren't what you think they should be, and you're in pain. Though this may, or even seem to be, the case, replace your words with hope, compassion, love, and encouragement. Not only does this apply to how you speak to others but also how you talk to yourself. Negative self-talk is useless and unproductive when you are working to better yourself or your life. For some, negative self-talk is viewed as a motivating factor or something that keeps them in-line. Though you may feel this way currently, it is not the truth. That idea is based on and comes from fear. Most people who do this type of self-talk and claim that it pushes them to do things are afraid that if they lighten up on themselves, they won't accomplish their goals or change anything they want to change. Ultimately, this has a substantial negative impact on your subconscious mind and is designed to keep you down in the end. If this were working for you, you probably wouldn't be reading this book. You wouldn't need to. This type of behavior is self-abuse and must be challenged and released if you want your life to improve. You may even feel as if the negative things you hear or say in your mind are right about you. You must challenge and release this type of thinking as well so you can begin to work from a place of empowerment.

You are human. You will make mistakes and poor choices in life sometimes. That is part of the human experience. It is something we all experience. This type of thinking is designed to keep you where you are because it is familiar, which is what the subconscious mind likes. As humans, we are creatures of habit. Even if where you are is painful, the comfort of being in this familiar place can override the pain of staying there versus the pain of changing. Create a new standard for yourself of not allowing those negative self-judgments and self-defeating thought patterns to continue. This may be difficult at first, but with repetition and perseverance, you will end this cycle and begin to take steps toward happiness and freedom in your life.

## The Impact of Your Environment

Let's talk about your environment for a moment. As I discussed in chapter two, about how your subconscious mind learns and accepts new programs, your environment provides consistent feedback to your mind. It's one of the primary reasons people tend to stay anxious or depressed. Your environment has a significant impact on your experiences. It is vitally important that your environment support the success you are seeking to achieve in your life. If you truly desire change in your life, you must create an environment that is conducive to the changes you want to make. If you are around people who are always worried and negative you will take on their worries and negativity. Many studies have shown that we take on the personalities and thinking patterns of those we associate with most. If you are around people who are depressed all the time, viewing their lives through a lens of doom and gloom, you too will begin or continue to see life similarly. Eventually, their perceptions will rub off on you, and you will be talking about how bad things are.

If you want to change, you must evaluate your environment and do your best to create one that is uplifting, encouraging, and supportive of your new goals. This can be a difficult shift for some people because they feel trapped where they are. They may have a partner like this whom they love very much or feel as if they're stuck in a situation with others they can't control. In this case, you must remain aware of the impact and do your best to speak words and create thought patterns that support your goal of living free and happy. You may even be surprised at how much you influence them to become free and happy as well. Negativity is dangerously contagious. If you have someone in your life who genuinely cares about you and knows you are trying to get better and live a different way, they will respect what you're trying to do and be understanding as well as supportive. People who genuinely care about you will always want the best for you, even if they don't agree with it or it feels like a loss for them.

This is also a time for you to begin setting boundaries, not just for others but also for yourself. If you are following the golden rules, then you have already started doing this. Setting boundaries and holding yourself accountable is the first step you must take. Then you can set healthy boundaries for how others treat you. Once you incorporate boundaries for yourself and begin living your life from these philosophies, you may find that you will outgrow some of the people in your life. I have seen some people outgrow friends, partners, and others, and they are more than happy about it.

When you live by the philosophies and teachings in this book, you will elevate your consciousness and state of being to higher levels than you can imagine from where you are right now in your life. As stated in Rule #2, if you want to see something new, you must become something new. When this happens and you transform your life, you may no longer be on the same level as the people or situations you are now around or in. This is a good thing because you will attract new friends, people, and conditions that you can relate to and enjoy on a level that supports the new you. Then your environment will help support who you want to be rather than who you have been. However, it will be your job to ensure that your environment remains that way. This can be difficult because letting people go from your life isn't always easy. They may not understand, or they may even feel rejected. It's important to realize that other people's feelings and experiences are not your responsibility. Your responsibilities are to regulate your thoughts, emotions, and actions and to make sure that your intentions come from a place of love and compassion for yourself and others. I've had to walk away from many people as I have grown, even family members, and still may have to do it in the future. This has been difficult at times, but it's what's right for me.

Some people may become envious of you for changing and leaving them behind, and they may even try to drag you back down to their level. Take this as a sign that you are on the right path. Don't let their words or actions take you down. It may be difficult at first, but as you grow and develop, those feelings will fade into distant memories. This may sound harsh, but it is necessary if you truly want the freedom and happiness you will gain in return. Sometimes you will only have to walk away for a season until you have healed, and sometimes you will find that they were only meant to be there for that season. You may have to go low or even no contact. Either way, you will be okay and much better off in the end.

## Control and Faith

For many people, the inability to control their external environment or situations can create states of anxiety. This primarily stems from a failure to create an internal state of stability. Typically, when people feel out of control or a sense of chaos within, they will try to control their external environment to induce a feeling or sense of stability and emotional calm. We see this a lot with people who suffer from OCD and control issues. While there's nothing wrong with having an organized environment or one that is structured, it will not provide long-term relief from anxiety or depression. It merely becomes a distraction that offers a false sense of security or emotional calm. Many people experience this, so it is necessary to address the issue of control.

Control is a major issue that many people have difficulty with, and it is rooted in fear. It's essential to understand what we can and cannot control. We don't control the unfolding of events or situations. We can't force people to behave in ways they don't want unless we use some form of manipulation or coercion. Doing this impedes on their free will and seeks to rob them of their power. Do you really want to deprive others of their power? Of course not. You want to feel better and may believe that your pain can only subside when the other person or situation changes. This is not, nor has it ever been, true. This can also be abusive behavior.

We can't control the course of events and how they unfold. That's not our job. Our job is to decide what we want in life and do what we can within ourselves to achieve it, not to control how it happens. If it is meant to happen, great. If not, great. If it's not meant to happen, you are probably better off in the end or will look back one day and be happy that it didn't. Some of the best things that have ever happened for me are things that I didn't want to happen. Don't get too caught up in the details. Allow yourself to flow with the currents of life. You will be okay. The future is always unpredictable, and that's okay. It must be okay because that's the way it is. This fact will not change, no matter how bad you may want it to. We must work within the system in which we exist. Trying to control the events of the future will only bring you pain and suffering. Do what you can do to take steps toward your goals and let life assist you the way it is designed to, by filling in all the details. This will bring everything together that you need to reach them. Some may be painful and others exciting. Nevertheless, everything is working on your behalf. Begin to have faith in life and yourself by conditioning your mind to recognize this principle.

When you set a goal, such as being free from anxiety and depression, you know where you are and where you want to be in life concerning that goal. Then you create a strategy on how you're going to get there. Your job is to decide which results you desire to produce and to take the steps you have created in your strategy. This is where your control ends. You can't control whether the steps you created will work or be successful in helping you achieve your goal. Each step you take will lead you to the next step of your process. Can you control or force it to unfold exactly the way that you had planned? No. This is something no one has ever been able to do. Once you have set the goal and created the strategy, your job is to take the steps and have faith in the process. If the steps you are taking begin to lead you away from your goal, you make the appropriate adjustments along your path to bring you back into alignment with your goal. You must have faith in this part of the process as well. You don't know exactly how this is going to happen or what experiences you will have throughout your journey. That's okay. Your job is to stay focused on the steps you are taking, nothing more. It is vital to your success that you understand what your role is and what it is not.

Not everything we do is going to be successful, nor should it be. Failure has a purpose. If everything happened exactly the way I wanted it to, I would not be where I am today. I would not have all the great things I get to have in my life now. Can you imagine everyone getting to dictate and decide how everything should happen? It would be chaos. We must come to some understanding that a supreme intelligence governs our existence. Whether you believe it is God, the universe, or whatever, there is something far greater at work than you and I. We must let go of the idea that we are in full control. This gets so many people in trouble, and I've seen devastating consequences from this type of thinking in people's lives as well as my own. If you were in control of how things turn out, you probably wouldn't be reading this book or need help with anxiety or depression—or anything else, for that matter.

We get to make choices in our lives that affect and influence things or people around us, but the ripple effect that stems from these things is beyond our control. If you're one of those people who seek to control yours or someone else's life, it is crucial to understand what you can control and what you cannot. It is not your job to understand or figure out the "hows" in life. A higher power presides over us all, putting all the pieces of our puzzle together. Letting go of control of how things are going to happen is essential to living a life of peace and freedom. I'm not speaking about strategy or planning. This book is all about strategy and planning. What I'm referring to is how all the pieces in life will come together. It is necessary to come to this understanding.

Wouldn't it be so freeing to know that you don't have to worry about controlling everything? Not having to make sure everything ends up how you think it should? Not having to deal with all the stress and worry of being right so that things turn out the way you want? And to not having to deal with controlling all the people who have another idea of how things should be or how to do them? I can assure you, it is. Control was one of my biggest issues in life. I pushed people away and damaged relationships, causing destruction and pain for other people I cared for deeply. Eventually, it brought me to my knees in despair. That's when I surrendered and began to live by faith. Faith is the sacred companion of the successful, happy, and free. Faith is the alternative and replacement for control.

To have faith means to have complete trust or confidence in someone or something. Faith is not some idea or concept. It is not a switch you can just turn on and off at will. Faith is a practice that is built through daily reinforcement. It is essential to have faith in the process in which you are now involved by investing yourself in it daily. Allow yourself the opportunity to experience hope through faith that this process will work for you just as it has worked for myself and many others. Many people believe they are different from everyone else, and while this or that may work for everyone else, it will not work for them. This is not true, nor is it a beneficial belief to continue holding on to. It's okay not to have 100 percent confidence and faith in this system in the beginning. As you see the compounding results you begin to produce in your life, your confidence and faith will increase. However, you must give your all to this process to experience the most beneficial effects possible.

Faith is sometimes viewed as an idea or a false sense of hope. Faith has measurable outcomes. It is very real and powerful. There have been many studies on the placebo effect and how a person's beliefs and faith can alter physical realities and experiences. This creates an energy that emits from a person and has a real impact on their experiences and manifestations. Having faith in something is developing a state of expectation for a specific experiential outcome. The stronger your faith is, the more powerful its effect. This is nothing more than pure science. It's also a law that governs humanity and has been talked and written about for thousands of years for a reason. I challenge you to have faith in this process you are investing in to eradicate anxiety and depression from your life. As you do the work, you will watch your life change profoundly.

# CHAPTER 5

# THE MODEL OF POWER

Empowerment is the key to overcoming anxiety and depression in your life. To be empowered means to stand in your personal power and pull from your strengths and the success qualities and characteristics built into your foundational settings. The truth is that you have more than enough strength to get through any situation or circumstance in your life and overcome anxiety and depression permanently. The problem comes when we disconnect from these core qualities of personal power within us and allow our circumstances and situations to define us. I call this the static of life. When you become empowered, you will face the struggles in your life and overcome them. You will no longer be afraid to make changes in your life or implement new strategies, and even if you do experience fear, it will not stop you. You will pull yourself from negative situations and keep yourself out of them. The first step to becoming empowered is through knowledge. Therefore, I am teaching you these philosophies and tools so you can empower yourself and become free from debilitation and lack of self-control. Let's begin with the Model of Power.

# Model of Power

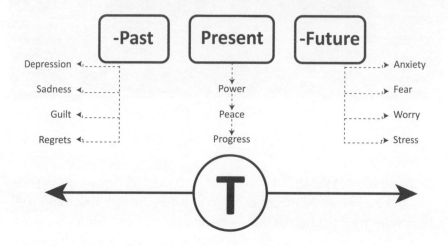

You can be in one of three mental states at any given time: past, present, or future. Each state has different properties and is the key to understanding where anxiety and depression stem from as well as their purpose. Everything you experience is in the present, but where your mental state is focused will determine what your experience will be.

Depression, sadness, guilt, and regret all have their roots in negative past-based thinking. They are results of thought patterns that are focused on past negative events, situations, outcomes, or ideas of your performance or actions that you either did or did not take. If you hang on to these negative thought patterns long enough, they can produce other dysfunctional emotional states such as shame, anger, and resentments. This happens when you identify with these past experiences and begin to judge yourself or others based on them. It is time to begin living your life with a new perspective on the past. Our pasts serve a great purpose for each of us. They are one of our greatest teachers. When we reflect on the past, both the good and bad outcomes, we can learn more about ourselves and the world around us. We can see how certain tendencies and strategies either help us progress further in life toward the things we truly desire or hold us back from ever having them. We can evaluate the effectiveness of our strategies and plan for the future more effectively.

There are so many gifts we can find when we stand in a healthy place and reflect on our pasts. When we're in our power, we don't become attached to what we've done or outcomes we have experienced in a disempowering way. Instead, we use the past to help us make necessary or beneficial adjustments and choices moving forward in our lives so we can create better results, change our outcomes, and step in-line with who we want to be. I'm sure there are many things you wish you had done or wanted to do but didn't for one reason or another. Maybe you missed a great opportunity or invested in a bad one. We all experience that because we're all human. It's part of being human. You have made mistakes and done things you knew were not good or right for yourself and others. Maybe you're not where you want to be in life and think you should be further ahead or somewhere else. Again, we all experience that because we're all human. Having those types of thought patterns is normal. Nevertheless, do not dwell in that place. It will not serve you. Reflect and adjust for a better future. Forgive and let yourself off the hook for your mistakes.

You cannot undo the things of the past, but you can change your approach and direction for a better future. Everything that has happened in the past is okay. It must be okay because it's already been done and you can do nothing to change it. If you focus on the past too much, you will bring it into your future through repeated cycles that cause you more pain and suffering. I'm not saying that everything you went through or that happened to you was right or acceptable. You may have been abused, mistreated, or wronged in a major way, and that is never acceptable. When I say that it is okay, I am speaking from a place of acceptance that this has been part of your experience in life and that it's time to come to peace with it so it doesn't hold you back any longer. What you focus on and give your attention to will determine the direction you will most likely move toward in your life. It will dictate what and who you are as well as what you experience. Furthermore, the past no longer exists. It is only a memory captured by your mind, and the only way you can experience it is through your thoughts. You cannot experience any of those things from your past outside of your own mind. If you want to end the cycles of depression in your life, you must stop investing your mental faculties into the negatives of your past.

Anxiety, fear, worry, and stress all stem from thought patterns focused on the negative uncertainties of the future, things that may or could happen that you either don't like or don't want to happen. The future is and will always be uncertain, just as it always has been. When we see higher levels of anxiety, fear, worry, and stress, we can always trace it back to lower levels of psychological security. This foundational system typically comes from the father or primary male figure in a child's life. It's time to begin living your life with a new perspective on the future. Mark Twain once said, "I've had a lot of worries in my life, most of which never happened."

The uncertainty of the future is a guarantee for each of us. It's just part of life. You don't know what's going to happen at any moment. If you're sitting down reading this book right now, I'll bet you don't even know exactly how you're going to get up. You may have an idea of what you will do, but until you do it, you can't be sure how everything will fall into place. What if your leg gives out or you lose your balance? What position will you even be in when you're ready to get up? What you do know is that you will find a way to stand up when the time comes. You will make whatever adjustments are necessary to ensure you stand up and get to your next destination. You don't know if the roads you usually travel down will be in working order when you go out later. Or if you're going to get that job. Or if that person is going to pull through on that promise made to you. Either way, no matter how it turns out and no matter what happens, good or bad, you will handle it when the time comes. You will find new roads, get another job, or find a way to make that something happen. You will, as you always have.

Now look at those answers you wrote down at the beginning of this exercise. When you brought your mental focus to a present state, all those emotional pains vanished and you no longer viewed these things as problems or something wrong but instead as situations in your life. The problems and suffering went away without the situations changing. This will give you some insight to begin realizing that problems exist only in our thinking and how we relate to them determines our experience with them (we will address this more in-depth in the upcoming chapters.)

This is the mental state where you will find and connect with your power and peace to make the greatest progress in your life. When you work from this state of empowerment, you can overcome and achieve anything you truly desire in your life. Conditioning your mind to be present focused will be the first part of your mental training. This may not be easy to accomplish at first, but with time and practice, you will stand in your power, live your life more effectively, and no longer be controlled by anxiety and depression.

When you bring your mental focus into the present moment, you will find that all those emotional pains vanish and you no longer view these things as problems or something wrong but instead as situations in your life. The problems and suffering went away without the situations changing. This will give you some insight to begin realizing that problems only exist in our thinking and how we relate to them determines our experience with them. (We will address this more in depth in the upcoming chapters.) This is the mental state where you will find and connect with your power and peace to make your greatest progress in life. When you work from this state of empowerment, you can overcome and achieve anything you truly desire in your life.

Now look at those answers you wrote down at the beginning of this exercise. You will find that they were only problems based on the way you were thinking of them. When you brought your mental focus to a present state, they were only situations or circumstances in your life. Conditioning your mind to be present focused will be the first part of your mental training. This may not be easy to accomplish at first, but with time and practice, you will stand in your power, live your life more effectively, and no longer be controlled by anxiety and depression.

It's time to understand that your emotional pain of anxiety and depression is there for a purpose. When you begin to use them for the purpose they're meant to serve, you can bring yourself back into your power and out of the pain. These emotional pains are not meant to hurt or harm you. They are not intended to disempower or defeat you. Most importantly, they are not the problem. As I explained in the pain versus pleasure principle, pain has a definite purpose. It is there to let us know there is a problem or conflict that needs to be resolved. The emotional pains of anxiety and depression are only indicators that you are out of your power by being mentally focused on the negatives of the past or future instead of the present moment.

People who are deeply invested in the negative results of their pasts will experience higher degrees of depression, sadness, guilt, or regrets that can lead to higher levels of shame, resentment, and anger. People who are deeply invested in possible negative outcomes of their futures will experience higher degrees of anxiety, fears, worries, or stress. The same principle and solution apply to each. I like to use the example of a patient visiting a doctor with shoulder pain. If the patient tells the doctor they have a sharp pain in their shoulder, he may first think to check the nerves in that area. If the patient tells the doctor they have a low, dull, or aching pain in their shoulder, he may first think to check the muscles in that area. The doctor will use the pain as an indicator to help him understand what the problem is.

Think of your emotional pain in the same way. If you begin to feel depressed or overwhelmed with sadness, your thoughts are focused on negative events or outcomes from the past. If you're dealing with anxiety or worries, your thoughts are focused on the negative possibilities of the future. These are indicators to let you know that you are out of your power, how and why you're out of your power, so that you can address the problem in your thinking. You may not be aware of your thoughts during these times, but when you bring your focus into the present state, you will begin to find relief.

# Truth

**I am resilient and can get through anything that comes my way in life; I always have.**

Is this statement true about you? The correct answer is a resounding *yes*! How do I know? Simple. If this weren't true for you, then you wouldn't be reading this book right now. Let's examine this statement a little more closely. I use the word *can* as it relates to getting through anything. This is speaking to your abilities, not your beliefs. Maybe you don't believe that you can get through something that is or may be coming your way in life, but the truth is that you have the ability. One of the most significant, effective shifts you will make in your life is to recognize and live based on your abilities rather than your beliefs. In other words, align your beliefs with your abilities, not your abilities with your beliefs. Your belief patterns are based on what you have learned or have seen throughout your life, which has formed your understanding of your limitations and identity.

Aligning your thought patterns with your abilities will undoubtedly free you from those mental prisons you have been living in and allow you the opportunity to change your experiences. The truth is that you do have the ability to get through anything that comes your way in life; you always have. You have gotten through everything you have ever been through in your life so far, all the big and small things, all the difficult and easy things, all the scary and calm things. *Everything.* Maybe you didn't get through them the way you wanted or would have liked to, but you did get through them, right? Of course you did. You found a way every time. This statement is as true for you now as it always has been and always will be. It is your default setting. It comes from the very substance that sustains your life.

There is only one event that you will not get through in your life, and that is your transition from human to spiritual—or what we call death. You are not supposed to get through this event, at least being human on the other side. But you will get through that one as well, just the way you're supposed to. Don't get too caught up in this final event, as it will rob you of the life you could be having in the present. That would be living outside of your power, in future-based thinking, which is sure to cause much emotional pain. As you acknowledge this statement as a truth for you, that you can get through anything that comes your way in life, just as you always have, what is there to truly worry about in the future? Sure, you may not know how things are going to work out for you, and you may be facing some challenges that you don't have a solution to or a plan for now, but one way or another, you will get through them and you will be okay. You always have, you always do, and you always will.

Truth is the primary tool or understanding that I will teach you to use as a filter in your life to help you live as an empowered person. Truth is a powerful force that can set you free to create peace and happiness in your life in every area and situation. But first it's essential to understand the context in which I talk about truth. Many people will say that the truth is different for each person. This is not an accurate statement. Facts may be different for different people, but the truth isn't. Facts are things to be known or proven to be accurate, but they are typically applied to situations, circumstances, events, and so forth. Facts can change as new knowledge is presented to support a case, but the truth will remain steady, no matter how many new facts enter the equation.

When I speak about truth, I am talking about universal truth—truth that goes beyond your situations. The truths I will be working with and helping you understand are the ones that each person who reads this book will resonate with. Understanding and incorporating truth will set you free and bring your life into higher levels of peace, happiness, and freedom. This guiding light will lead you to your personal power, where you can make the changes you truly desire to make. It will help you rebuild the core foundations that guide your life, such as psychological security, self-esteem, confidence, and strength. It will shine a light on all the lies you have been carrying around for many years, which have and are causing you most of the emotional pain you experience in your life.

Let me ask you a question. If someone close to you had been lying to you for years, maybe even your entire life, and you found out, could you believe that lie again, even if they begged you to? Of course you couldn't. You couldn't possibly unknow that you knew it was a lie. What if that person was you? As far-fetched as this may sound, as you learn and implement the tools and techniques I teach in this book, you will see that you've been lying to yourself about many things in your life that have caused you so much pain and suffering. But you're not responsible for putting all those lies into your mind. They came from your environment and upbringing as you learned about life throughout your years on earth. Once you have revealed the lies and the truth, you will never again believe those lies. A phenomenal transformation will take place within you at that very moment, altering the course of your life.

As you begin to implement this into your life, you will find yourself indulging in future- and past-based thinking at times. You will make mistakes. Each time you catch yourself, praise yourself and shift your thoughts. Do not beat yourself up. I repeat, do not beat yourself up. You are programmed to think the way you do, and it will take some time to implement this new mental training for it to become automatic. Be patient and kind to yourself. If you are not, the process will take much longer.

When you find yourself indulging in thoughts of negative possible future outcomes and you experience anxiety, remember the truth about you—that you are resilient, that you can and will get through anything and everything that comes your way in life, just as you always have.

When you find yourself indulging in negative outcomes from the past and you experience depression, remember that your identity and who you are is not fixed and that you can change your life and experiences. The past does not bind your future or even your present but instead serves as a teacher to help you improve yourself and your situations if you have the courage and discipline to use the lessons you have learned and apply them to your life in the present. Use your pain to understand and correct the problem so you can begin to live free from debilitating anxiety and depression. It's okay to experience low levels of anxiety and sadness from time to time. They can help you grow and prepare in many helpful ways in life. Experiencing these symptoms is not the problem. Staying in them is. Use the Model of Power and the processes in the upcoming chapters to discover the truth to help you identify and eliminate your emotional pain. Keep these teachings in the front of your mind until they are deeply embedded into your subconscious and become automatic. Remember, this is mental training; it will take time, effort, and consistency.

# CHAPTER 6

# SETTING GROWTH GOALS

Change and growth follow the law of process, just as everything does. Change does not necessarily lead to growth, but growth always leads to change. If you want something new in your life, you must become something new. There's no way around this. Growth is a process that takes time, discipline, and consistency. It is not an elevator that takes you straight to the top. It's like peeling the layers from an onion. When you've successfully peeled one layer and resolved the conflict within it, you will begin to peel another layer to resolve the conflict within it, and so on. As you grow, you will encounter difficulties and struggles.

I always say that when we are asking for growth or higher levels in life, we are asking for trouble. The struggles we go through are designed to shape and mold us into greater beings to do greater things. Several formulas are floating around for setting goals to attain different results in our lives. A lot of them are great tools and can be beneficial, but most lack the necessary ingredients to create and sustain long-term change as it applies to anxiety and depression.

People tend to weigh themselves down with structures and lists that go on and on. This is not an effective strategy to get rid of anxiety and depression but instead serves to distract the person's mind enough to give them a false sense of progress because they have become dependent on movement and action to create a sense of psychological security and stability within themselves. If you want to remove these cycles from your life, it's time to begin taking a more practical approach to your goals of clearing out anxiety and depression.

# Who(Growth)

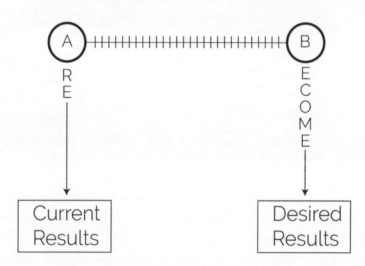

Most people relate to goal setting as where they are (point A) and where they want to be (point B). They base this on external factors and set their goals accordingly. An example of this could be easily seen with those on a yo-yo dieting cycle. They determine they want to lose fifty pounds, so they set that as their goal. They put a plan of action in place to begin their diet and exercise routine. Typically, they stay on track for a few weeks, until they encounter the terror barrier and face the old programs trying to survive this change. This is when they begin to lose their motivation and discipline and resort to fast-tracking their goals. They may take some dietary supplements or do something to render the results more quickly.

Once they reach their goal, their actions and behaviors begin slipping back into old patterns. Before long, they are back to where they stepped out of the process and they lose the results they began working toward. When they feel enough pain from the weight again, they step into the same cycle, sometimes in a different way, to see if the next strategy will work for them. Some people will repeat this pattern many times, thus called the yo-yo dieter. Let's look at a more practical approach to setting and reaching goals that will help you in your journey of dissolving anxiety and depression from your life.

You first need to understand the difference between a goal and an outcome. Using the weight loss example above, suppose a person sets their goal to lose fifty pounds. That is not a goal but instead an outcome that reaching the goal produces. Your goal should never be the outcome. Deciding on the outcome you wish to create is necessary but is only the effect or result of reaching your goal. A more effective approach is to gain clarity on who you need to be to create the results you want and work to become that version of yourself. Who you are being determines what you create and produce in life. By changing who you're being, you will automatically change the results and be able to sustain them. To do this, we must change our understanding of the whole system. You must realize that point A and point B are not where you are and where you want to be but instead who you are and who you must become to produce those outcomes you desire. I often say that we don't get in life what we want; we get in life what we are.

The reason people attract different things is because they are different in who they are or are being. In most cases, it's not a matter of situations and circumstances, though it may appear that way. For example, think about people who grew up in poverty. They may have taken on beliefs and understandings related to money from their environment and upbringing, that money is hard to come by or money is a struggle. That belief system keeps them in situations that reinforce it. To change this, they must become the version of themselves that has a healthy relationship with money. By doing so, they will find more or better opportunities to improve their financial circumstances. In the example of weight loss, the goal should be to become the people they need to be to create and sustain less weight. They must become people who enjoy taking care of their bodies, exercising, eating healthy, and loving themselves. When they become those people, they will make healthier decisions for themselves which can help them create and sustain the results they want.

Your goal should always be growth oriented, not action oriented. This doesn't mean that action will not be required as part of your process, but instead, the action you take must lead to outgrowing the version you are now, who produces the results you currently have in your life. This is the key to creating change in your life long term. Who you are being will determine every aspect of your life. If you want something different, you must become something different. Your action must lead to personal growth. Otherwise, you may fall into the same trap of insanity, chasing temporary relief and only producing temporary results.

To set a growth goal, decide what type of person or experience you will be and have when you create the results you prefer in your life. What qualities and characteristics will you exude? How will you conduct yourself in different situations in your life? Once you determine who you will become and how you will live your life, begin to work on growing into that type of person or that version of yourself. Then you will start to create those results in your life. Many people say, "I'll believe it when I see it." However, you'll only see it when you believe and become it. This is the way it works. You will only create and sustain results in your life when you become the person you need to be to create and sustain them. Begin to expand your mind and act based on the growth goals you set for yourself, even when you don't see the results yet. Once you have achieved higher levels of growth in your life, you will create greater experiences and results for yourself.

## Process versus Result Orientation

Now that you understand more clearly how to set your goals based on growth, it's time to focus on the process of growth. One of the biggest mistakes people make when pursuing their goals is that they become results oriented. They focus on the results they want to create so much that they lose focus on the process. One of the keys to staying in your power and achieving the results you want will come through being process oriented rather than result oriented. Being process oriented means focusing on where you are in your process of growth rather than the outcome. All results are created through a process. This is true for every result you will ever produce or create in your life. Once you create the goal based on an understanding of what growth must occur to deliver the results you want, you should focus most of your attention on the process. If you want faster results, become more focused on the process. If you want to create results that are more effective, make sure you are managing each step of the process fully.

The process of staying focused on the present, discussed in chapter five, applies to the process of growth as well. Staying present in the process allows you to manage each step effectively so you can progress to the next step. You will reach your goal one single step at a time. Do not try to skip steps or you'll end up like the yo-yo dieter. The only way to get to your goal is to take each step and adequately manage it. Growth happens organically. There's an ebb and flow to it. If you want to speed it up, focus on managing your current step as effectively as possible. This is important for you to know and understand.

When you're trying to manage the previous steps you took, you will not be able to manage the one you're in sufficiently. Focusing on your past while trying to achieve your goal will cause you to get off course, stumble, and go through unnecessary pain and suffering. This can be avoided if you manage where you are instead of where you've been. It can also cause you to sabotage your goal. We move toward the things we focus on in life, so if you're focusing on the past, you are more likely to recreate those same experiences for yourself in the future. You can't manage the steps from your past. They are done. It's time to re-center your focus on where you are, make whatever adjustments are necessary to take you where you want to go, and allow the lessons you learned from the past to help you better manage the present and future.

This same principle applies when looking too far ahead. When you're trying to manage steps that are ahead of you before you get there, you are setting yourself up for unnecessary pain and suffering. You cannot manage the steps ahead of you from where you are. If you manage the step you're in adequately, you will be prepared for your future steps. It's okay to peak into upcoming steps of the process you're in for preparation purposes, but don't focus on them. Focus your attention on where you are and managing that step. When you do this, it will lead you to the next step, and the next, and so on.

Earlier I discussed the truth of your resilience. You are resilient and can get through anything that comes your way in life; you always have. Here's where you need to focus on this truth about yourself. As you stand in your power in the present moment where you currently are in your process, remember that you will handle and take care of anything that comes your way in the future. You will be okay, and you will make it through. You know this because you always have. You may not like every step, and you may have some struggles or difficulties that cause you pain and suffering. Nevertheless, you will make it through. You will learn valuable lessons, and you will grow through it, if you allow yourself. No matter what you experience, you will overcome the challenges in your future. You will find a way. Remember, this is your default setting. When you foresee any danger or threat in your future, you can begin to manage yourself where you are in the process of preparing yourself and your life for the best possible outcome. But again, you can only do this in the present moment. This is where your power is. The further outside of the present moment you are, the more emotional pain you will experience to let you know to shift your focus and attention to the present moment and step back into your power.

At this point in your process, your goal should not be to overcome anxiety or depression, but instead to effectively overcome the thought processes creating these experiences by training your mind to stay focused in the present moment. When you learn to master each moment, you will gain freedom from anxiety and depression. The result will be no longer experiencing debilitating anxiety and depression; the goal for you is to grow into the version of yourself who doesn't. This happens one step at a time. You cannot skip steps in a growth goal. It simply will not work. Focus on each moment as it comes, with your mind set on managing and regulating your thought processes and emotional responses. Remember, the brain learns through repetition. By repeating this process consistently, you are teaching your brain to think and respond differently. When you focus on the results you seek from where you currently are, you will most assuredly become overwhelmed because at this point you can't possibly fathom thinking or responding in a more effective way than you do now. It may even sound foreign to you at this point, but in time, you will have reprogrammed your mind in such a way that anxiety and depression will no longer be a typical experience for you. In the next chapter, I will teach you more about how to achieve this.

# CHAPTER 7

# THE PROCESS OF GROWTH

As you set growth-based goals to overcome anxiety and depression in your life, it's essential to understand what the process of growth looks like. Many people view growth as a steady progression that turns into a momentum that becomes self-sustaining. While growth can create more growth, it's not exactly cut-and-dried. When people are growing mentally, emotionally, or spiritually, they will encounter what seems like setbacks. At times, it may feel as if they're moving two steps forward and three steps back. This is when most people forsake their goals and return to past behaviors and mindsets.

Growth is a process, just like anything else in life. Some days will be tougher than others, while some will be easier. When you invest yourself in growth-based goals, you will most certainly experience discomfort. You must become comfortable with this discomfort if you want to succeed. If you're suffering from anxiety and depression, you are already uncomfortable, so make it worth it by becoming comfortable with the changes taking place. Old things will arise in your mind, giving you every opportunity to support the old program by justifying why you should stay where you are in life or why you should repeat those old behaviors and patterns of thought. Growth is organic and will happen as fast and to the degree in which you are ready and allow it. When you invest in your growth, your old programs will try to manipulate you into sabotaging yourself in a variety of ways. Understanding the terror barrier, how it works, why it's there, and how to overcome it is essential to move through them and achieve the growth you are seeking.

# The Terror Barrier

Change can be a difficult process for people to go through. As I mentioned previously, the subconscious mind doesn't like to change. It prefers to run the programs it has, and that's it. When replacing programs in the subconscious mind, you will encounter the terror barrier. Imagine the programs in your mind as living entities. They live and breathe inside of you, and they want to stay alive just as any living entity does. They feed on the energy you supply them through reinforcing the same habits and thought patterns. When they feel their life is in danger because you begin to feed the new programs you are working to install, they will fight for survival. Every living creature does this.

If you were in danger, wouldn't you fight to stay alive any possible way you could? Of course you would. People have been known to go to extremes to ensure their survival. The survival technique subconscious programs use to stay alive is what we call the terror barrier. This is nothing to fear. When you encounter it, it's because you are on the verge of a breakthrough. Understanding it in this way can help you feel good even though you may be experiencing difficulties because you know something great is about to happen: change. Let's discuss the terror barrier in detail.

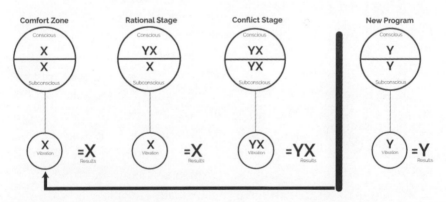

We begin with the comfort zone. This state occurs when the input you receive from external sources through your senses matches the dominant programs within your subconscious mind. We'll call this program "X." This creates a vibrational frequency in the body that matches the program, which then creates your results and experiences accordingly. The vibrational frequency is an energy that you emit from your being that works to attract and create external experiences.

When new information enters the conscious mind that is different or unlike the program X, you move into the rational stage. We'll call this new input program "Y." In the rational stage, your conscious mind will be looking for reinforcement as to whether the new program, Y, is suitable or beneficially serving your needs. This process is taking place within your mind as you learn these philosophies and more about yourself. In this stage, this new information has not penetrated the subconscious mind so you continue to emit a vibrational frequency consistent with X program and produce results and experiences accordingly. With enough reinforcement in the rational stage to support the new program Y, it begins to move into the subconscious mind. This is where the difficulty can begin. Now you have opposing programs in the subconscious mind that are battling it out. I call this duality. Each will fight for survival. This is the conflict stage. It disrupts the normal flow of program X, and you begin to emit a mixed vibrational frequency and produce mixed results. This is where the terror barrier kicks in.

The terror barrier is the defense system of the more dominant program and is designed to kill off the new program you are working to install. In this stage, you will experience the sometimes harsh effects of the terror barrier. Since it's a program of the mind, that's where you can expect the battle to be. You may experience fear, resistance, lack of motivation, guilt, or loss of enthusiasm, among many other things that can make you feel disempowered. It will lie to you and flood you with emotions to lure you back into your old patterns and experiences. Its strategy is to push you back to the original comfort zone and eradicate the new program. This very effective strategy works most of the time on people who are unaware of this process and its nature.

A great example of this occurring is at the beginning of a new year with people who set goals to change their life is some way. They build themselves up for a great year of releasing the old and bringing in the new. At first, they're all in. They feel motivated and determined as they step into action. After the third week, most people have fallen off the wagon and forsaken the goals and visions they had for themselves. They lose their motivation to continue doing the work, and they fall back into the same patterns they had before. Then they make excuses as to why they couldn't continue, such as not having enough time or that they didn't care about it much to begin with.

What happened? They hit the terror barrier, and it took them back to the comfort zone. Even though being in the comfort zone is not comfortable to them, it is easier to stay or return there than to continue moving forward to break through the terror barrier and create the results they wanted. The terror barrier takes place about three weeks into change for most people but can vary from person to person. I tend to experience a terror barrier around three months into changing a program. If you want to change the program and experience new results in your life, you must push through the terror barrier. To do this, you must continue your journey and fight through the effects of the terror barrier by staying as focused as possible on your present and the truth, not the pain. You also must be able to discern the difference between the lies and manipulation in your mind versus the truth and your desire. I will teach you the processes of discernment to help overcome the terror barrier when it hits. This is easier said than done, but it's necessary if you want things to change in your life. Once you break through the terror barrier, you will step into a new comfort zone running the new program, "Y."

Whenever change happens, you will go through some level of the terror barrier. One way to make this easier on yourself is to reflect on your life and try to notice when you may have encountered the terror barrier and how it affected you. It will typically use the same strategy each time. Maybe there was a goal that you decided on and somehow found yourself walking away from it. What did you experience during that time? Did you lose your motivation? Did you suddenly change your mind? Gaining insight into how you experience the terror barrier will allow you to plan and know what to expect when it comes up. I tend to experience a lack of motivation and a loss of enthusiasm when I encounter the terror barrier. Once I recognize what's happening, I quickly get back in touch with what it is I genuinely want, align my thoughts with the truth, and allow myself to put my feelings aside. Again, this is easier said than done, but it is possible for you as well through mental training.

As you implement the philosophies and tools in this book, you may find yourself facing the terror barrier. It may bring additional anxious thoughts or depression after a few weeks to entice you to forsake your new thought patterns and behaviors. You may find yourself losing focus and not following through on the exercises. Remember why this is happening and don't give in! By staying focused and committed, you will soon see change taking place in your life in a profound way. Know that it's just a tactic of your old program trying to survive and that it will do anything it can to succeed.

## One Step at a Time

Every result follows the law of process. To create the change from debilitation to freedom most effectively, you must take one single step at a time. This means you must manage where you are in the process at all times. Do not get ahead of yourself and try to rush to the results to get rid of the pain and distress you are experiencing. As counterintuitive as this may sound, doing so will extend your healing time, or worse yet, keep you from healing. You must learn to follow the process one step at a time so you can effectively manage it. At first, this may feel abnormal because you're not used to thinking this way. As you waver in and out of your power, you will have many moments when you may feel that you can't do this. Remember the truth at these moments. And the truth is that you can do this. It may be difficult, but you do have the ability to change your thinking. You may become frustrated; that's okay. Just bring your mind back to the present by remembering that you can overcome anything that comes your way in life, even if it's difficult. Be patient with yourself. Again, this is mental training, and it's not going to happen overnight.

One little trick I use is a process called "chunking down." This means breaking down time into smaller and more manageable bits. For example, if my mind begins to worry about a situation in the future that I can't do anything about now, I will put it off in my mind and permit myself to think about or indulge in it later. I may say to myself, "Just for today, I will focus on the present, and tomorrow I will allow myself to think and worry about it then." When tomorrow comes, I just rinse and repeat. If this is too much, I may break it down into smaller chunks and say that I will allow myself to think about it in an hour, but for now I am going to focus on what I am doing and what's happening in my present. At the end of the hour, I rinse and repeat.

Chunking down your time into smaller, more manageable bits can relieve a lot of stress and feelings of being overwhelmed in this undertaking. If you find another way that works well for you to achieve this, use it. The objective is to make this practical so you can use it in your life to achieve the results you want. This does not mean ignoring real problems or discarding planning for the future. If a potential problem could arise in the future and you can prepare for it in the present, make the preparations. Ignoring problems doesn't make them disappear. Many problems in life are because of poor planning and preparation. Do what you can do in the present to prepare for such things, be okay with knowing you have done all you can at this moment, and let go of the worries of the future, knowing that you will handle and get through whatever comes your way, just as you always have.

# CHAPTER 8

# ACCEPTANCE

To change anything in your life, you must come to accept the way it is and your part in it. Is it okay for you to be where you are right now in your life? Who you are right now? With the tendencies you have right now? Experiencing life the way you are right now? Yes. It must be because it's where and who you are. You are currently a product of your past programming and choices. Right now everything is what it is. This doesn't mean that you like the way things are but instead that you accept the realities of your current state of life.

You have two choices you can make with this information. One, you can indulge in the emotional pain brought on by your circumstances and state of being and allow them to keep you there. I'm sure your mind can give you many great reasons why you should choose to do this, but remember that your mind is running a program that put you where you are and is designed to keep you there. Or two, you can choose to recognize that this is where, who, and what you are currently but that you can change and create new and better circumstances for yourself. Option two gives you the power to change your future for the better. You may have always been this way, and your mind may tell you that it's just who you are, but your program is only based on what you've learned throughout life. If your mind is telling you this, I have a simple question to ask you: do you have the ability to learn new things? Absolutely! This means you can learn new ways of handling and managing life that bring you happiness, fulfillment, and peace—new ways that will take you further than ever before.

I talk about truth a lot and will be teaching you new methods of discovering the truth in your life. This is just another one to add to your list of truth statements: you can learn all the things you need to learn to achieve all the things you want to achieve. And this truth applies to learning new strategies for living your life more effectively, without debilitating anxiety or depression.

Everything you have done is done. The past will try to hold you captive, but remember what the past is for: to learn and grow from. It's time to forgive yourself, and you have full permission to accept yourself for all the things you have been beating yourself up over and all the mistakes you have made. It doesn't matter how bad or wrong it was. It is done and over with. You cannot change or solve it now. Problems of the past don't even exist anymore. Only the effects of them exist. You must let go of them so you can move forward more healthily and effectively. You are learning new skills and shifting your paradigm so you don't do those same things you did in the past. What you did was based on what you learned and were programmed to do. With the new programs you are working to create through these teachings, you can use the lessons from your past and turn them into blessings for yourself and others in the future.

Nothing you have done or experienced in life is unforgivable, and everything that has been done to you can be forgiven as well. When you forgive others, you're not allowing them permission or a free pass. Instead, you're letting yourself off the hook from being tied down to those things. You may even be in a legal battle over something that someone did to you. Forgiving them doesn't mean walking away; it just means that you've accepted that these things have happened but they will not control or determine your destiny and how you experience life anymore. Great freedom and peace can come from acceptance and forgiveness. When you hold on to things, they control you and dictate your experiences. This isn't fair or even necessary for you, but it's how it works. You can choose now to accept and release yourself so you can break free from those chains that have held you back from the life you deserve to live.

Maybe you have many flaws or feel you lack the characteristics that would make you the type of person you want to be. We all experience this because it's part of being human. Accept yourself fully for who you are and everything about yourself. When you reject aspects of yourself, they become shadow parts that will follow you around and cause chaos in your life. You must begin to have the courage to look at these things so that you can work on them. This is how you change them. Rejecting these unwanted parts and aspects of yourself or your life doesn't make them go away or disappear; instead, it makes them worse.

It's when we dare to look at ourselves for what and who we are that we can create change. This begins with accepting yourself fully, right here, right now. When you dare to face your internal demons, you will find the strength to defeat them. Every problem has a solution. Starting now, begin to stand in your power and recognize that you can overcome and change these things about yourself. You are human, and you will make mistakes. You do have the ability to learn new ways of being and experiencing life, starting from where and who you are right now. This is where you begin because this is where you are. It's not a bad place to be. It's just not where you want to be. To stand in your power, you must be fully present. This means accepting everything that you are and everything that is. Then, and only then, can you effectively change who you are and what you are experiencing in life.

Let's try a little exercise. I'm going to ask you a question, and I want you to take a moment to write down your answer on a sheet of paper before proceeding. What's wrong with you as a person? Take your time and write everything down you can think of. Many people will begin with a list of things they believe is wrong with them. Can I tell you something that may surprise you? The answer to this question is *nothing*! There is nothing wrong with you. You are not broken. You are not a bad person. You are not wrong for feeling and experiencing life the way you do. You must first realize this.

What you are experiencing may be difficult, but it does not define who you are unless you allow it to. It does not mean that something is wrong with you. If something were wrong with you as a person, then you would be stuck with the results and experiences you have because you are stuck with you. But you already know that you are not stuck with the results and experiences you have in your life right now. You may feel stuck at this point, but as you work through this mental training, you will change your experiences. What you are experiencing is a result of your subconscious programming. Through this process, you will be able to change your subconscious programming to one that is more effective and beneficial, one that serves you in a better and more desirable way.

Imagine a table in front of you with all your characteristics, troubles, tendencies, actions, and responses in life on it. As you sift through each of them, you notice the things that are and are not serving you the way you would like them to in your life. You may think, *This thing isn't working well for me, and that one is good; but this one isn't serving me, and I'd like to change it.* The things that are not serving you well or are keeping you stuck in life can be changed or altered in ways that will serve you better in the future. These things are not part of who you are. They are only the things you are doing and experiencing. They are separate from your identity and can be changed when the right type of work is performed. These challenges are not bigger than you are. They are only aspects of your experience in life brought on and sustained by your subconscious programming.

The biggest problems come when people begin to identify with the things they have done, mistakes or decisions they have made, or things about themselves that they don't like. Your identity is not fixed. It can change. If it were true that something was wrong with you as a person, this would not be the case, and you would be wasting your time trying to help yourself. If this were true, I would not have written this book due to being who I used to be. I think we can agree that even though you may not have found the answer to your pain yet, that it is possible to change it. Allow yourself to release these limiting beliefs about yourself. They will not serve you well in any area of your life. Is this scary? Of course! Change can be scary because it takes us out of our comfort zones. If you want to change these things, you will have to face the fear of change. Do not identify with your past behaviors or outcomes. When you do this, you place a label on yourself that governs your existence in this world.

If you walk around with an identity that says that you're nothing, what do you think you will create in your life? The answer is a lot of situations and circumstances of worthless things and outcomes that reinforce that you are nothing. Who you are at the core of your being is perfect and beautiful. Being perfect does not mean you do everything perfectly or flawlessly. Flawlessness doesn't exist in human nature, and it would be foolish to hold yourself to an entirely impossible standard. You are human. That means you will make mistakes, cause troubles for yourself and others at times, make foolish decisions, and suffer sometimes. Be human and accept yourself for all your flaws and imperfections. It's okay.

Right now, at this very moment in time, you are taking steps in your process of growth. The first thing you must do to be successful is accept yourself and everything that is part of this step. Accepting everything means that you are willing to face these things so you can overcome them and move your life in a new direction. Do not reject anything. Acknowledge the negative behaviors, tendencies, and parts of yourself and allow them to be okay. This doesn't mean to continue doing the things that are keeping you where you are. You have a choice when you allow yourself to accept. You can choose to continue with that behavior and create those unwanted circumstances in your life or you can remember that you can get through anything in your life because you are resilient, making the necessary adjustments to your thinking and behaviors.

You may have specific thought patterns that in the past may have caused you to act impulsively. That's okay. Accept that your mind thinks the way it does and then acknowledge that you can change how you respond to it. You have control over how you respond to the thoughts in your mind. This may not be easy at first, but after some time of training your mind through using the filter of truth, you will find those thought patterns changing into ones that are more aligned with your power, which will create higher emotional states, drive more effective actions, and create positive changes in your life.

## Expectation versus Reality

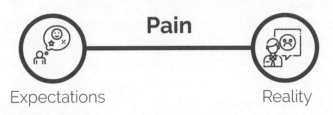

A significant point of pain that many people experience in life comes from their expectations of where they should be or what they thought would be or happen versus the reality and truth of how things are. It's crucial to align your expectations with truth and reality if you want to avoid this type of pain and suffering. Life is unpredictable. We never really know what's going to happen until it happens, for we are not designed to know. When we try to overcompensate for the lack of psychological security by creating expectations and ideas of what or where we think we should be or what should happen, we tend to feel the pain of the difference between our expectations and the reality. A belief system that serves me well and helps me overcome this type of thinking and avoid this type of pain is that I am where I am meant to be, going through what I'm meant to go through, at all times. This is a belief system that there is always a purpose to the pain I experience and that my job is to figure out what that purpose is and grow from it. This helps me shift my thoughts from the perceived problem to the lesson I am meant to learn and grow through to become better.

I believe that every situation and circumstance has something to offer that will help me become better in some way that I am meant to become better in. This comes from the understanding I have gained that everything in life is a gift, even the negative feeling things. When we step into this type of mindset, we begin to see life in an entirely new way. As with all things, you must implement this practice daily to make it a permanent belief if you want to enjoy the benefits it will bring you. This is just another way of accepting things as they are instead of diving into the rabbit hole and losing yourself in the emotional experiences you don't want to have. This will allow you to look for and see the opportunities and possibilities that could be presented to help you grow or change something that doesn't serve you well. Remember, the pain has a purpose; when we outgrow the patterns and behaviors that cause them, the pain will go away.

Stepping fully into acceptance and aligning your thoughts with reality and truth rather than relying on your expectations can help you avoid the pain and suffering that can often follow this way of thinking. This doesn't mean to release all your expectations in life. I have many for myself, but when I become aware of any pain coming from the misalignment between these two, I quickly step back into acceptance, faith, and the truth that I am where I am meant to be at all times, and I will be okay no matter what comes my way because I am resilient. This allows me to plan or create a strategy to move from where I am to where I want to be, but with the understanding that I had to go through whatever I went through for some greater purpose. Once I do this, I release it and continue staying present-minded and accepting of where I am, knowing this was all part of the process I was meant to go through to grow to a higher state of being. Being where you are at all times is okay. It may not feel good, but it is okay to be there, regardless of where you are. Becoming okay with it will lessen and sometimes completely release the struggle so you can address and change the program that created it.

## Shifting Your Focus

Let's do a little experiment. Try with all your might not to think of a green apple. Put all your effort into it. No matter how hard you try, you simply can't. The harder you try, the more you do. As with shadow parts, the more you resist, the more they persist. This is a fundamental understanding you need to learn about the subconscious mind. It doesn't respond to what you like and don't like or what you do or do not want. It responds to your focus. When you focus on something, you feed it. And what you feed will always grow. Getting rid of thoughts or things you don't want in life will not happen through resistance, only acceptance. This may sound counterintuitive, but it's the way the subconscious mind works. Let's try this again but in a slightly different way. Do your best not to think of a green apple. Try as hard as you can. Doesn't seem to be working, huh? Now shift your focus to the present moment. Look around the room or environment you are in. Take notice of the details. Stay there for just a moment. What happened to the green apple? It disappeared all on its own.

When you were trying to force it out of your mind, you were feeding it through focus, thus holding it in place. When you shifted your focus, you allowed it to leave. This is the key. Your mind is currently conditioned to focus on the past and future, which feeds the emotional pain you experience in the form of anxiety and depression. Allow this to be okay and shift your focus to the present moment. If you focus on negative future- or past-based thoughts, you will continue to create more of them. Don't fight or try to get rid of them. If you do, you will feed them. Each time you shift your focus from the past and future to the present, you are reconditioning your mind. This takes time and consistency.

If your mind drifts into the negatives of the future 1,000 times today, shift your focus to the present moment 1,001 times. If your mind drifts into the negatives of the past 1,000 times today, shift your attention to the present moment 1,001 times. Each time you do, it's like doing another curl-up in the gym, and that mental muscle will grow stronger. When you have reconditioned your mind, it will primarily stay focused on the present moment, where you will find a whole new level of life and experiences happening for you. It's quite magical. However, you must be persistent and diligent.

When the negative future-based thoughts come in and you experience fears, worries, anxieties, and stress, remember that you are resilient and that you can and will get through whatever comes your way in life, just as you always have. There's nothing you can't handle. Then allow them to be there and shift your focus to the present moment and continue with your life. When the negative past-based thoughts come up and you begin to experience depression, sadness, guilt, or regrets, remember that your future will be different as you open yourself up to new ways of living that are far greater than anything you have experienced in your past. Then allow those thoughts to be there and shift your focus to the present moment and continue with your life. Remember, they are just thoughts. They cannot harm or control you without your permission. You have had millions of thoughts throughout your life that you didn't respond to. You can do this. Make this a top priority for your life and watch it change profoundly.

## Putting the Process into Practice

When people ask me how long this mental training process takes, I usually respond with, "If you are twenty feet into hell, you still have to walk twenty feet to get out of hell." However long it takes you to put these teachings into practice—and to the degree that you do so— will affect the time it takes to begin creating experiences of peace and happiness. I typically see dramatic changes in people just after the first week of implementing these teachings when they make it a top priority. The first step is to understand the purpose of the emotional pains you are experiencing and to use them accordingly. If you are experiencing depression, sadness, guilt, or regret, you are focusing your mental faculties on the negative thoughts of the past. If you are experiencing anxiety, fear, worry, or stress, you are focusing your mental faculties on possible negative outcomes of the future.

The purpose of these pains is to help you identify where your mental focus is and to move back into the present moment, where your power is. I often say that these pains are telling you to mind your business, and your business is always in the present. When you notice your thoughts drifting to other mental states in a negative way or you feel these emotional pains, shift your focus back into your present moment and praise yourself for the growth you just made. Do not beat yourself up for slipping. It's all part of the process. Do not expect this to be easy at first. If you begin beating yourself up, stop immediately and praise yourself for changing that self-talk. If your mind goes to the past negatives, acknowledge it and accept that it is okay and that you are now on your way to changing your future. Then shift your focus to the present and praise yourself. If your mind goes to the future negatives, remember the truth about your resilience and ability to get through anything that may come. Then shift your focus to the present and praise yourself. Remember, this is a process. Do not get caught up in the results of peace and relief you are working to create in your life but rather the step of the process of growth you are currently in. This is the quickest way to attain those results.

Accept everything that is part of this step, even though it may be painful at this moment. Stay focused on the present as much as possible and know that you are on your way to a much better experience in your life. Follow the golden rules, each of them. Implement these teachings throughout each day and night and begin to filter your thoughts through the lens of truth. Each week recheck your scores on the Burns Depression Checklist and the Burns Anxiety Inventory to measure your progress. Remember the terror barrier and expect it to arise due to your programs being challenged and replaced. Do your best, take one step at a time, accept your mistakes, and stay focused, knowing that as you do, change will inevitably happen for you.

# PART III

## THE TOOLS AND TECHNIQUES

As you begin standing in your power, it's critical to understand what experiences are and how they are created so you can remain in your power. This knowledge will give you great power in understanding how to change them as well. Most people look outside themselves to improve the experiences they have in life. This is not an effective long-term strategy because one will typically end up with different circumstances while creating a relatively similar experience. Previously, I talked a little about how events do not create experiences but instead our internal representations, associations, and relationships with them. Now it's time to dive deeper to understand the process of experiences and, more importantly, how to change them.

## The Model of Human Experience

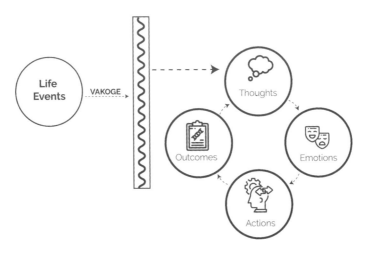

Most people think they are experiencing the events in their lives through situations, circumstances, things, and so forth, but the reality is that we don't experience anything outside of us. You have never had an external experience, and you never will. We have six ways of collecting data from the outside world. We refer to these as VAKOGE (visual—sight, auditory—sound, kinesthetic—motion, olfactory—smell, gustatory—taste, energetic—energy). When external data comes in through one or more of our six senses, such as seeing or hearing an event in life outside of our bodies, it processes through the subconscious mind. This acts as a filtration system that processes the data through past learnings, understandings, and foundational settings to give it meaning or value so that we can interpret the data. The interpretation comes from the relationship or association we have learned about the external data. The interpretation of the data produces a thought pattern that flows into the conscious mind for us to become aware of in order to sift through it and apply it to us or our surroundings in the most appropriate way.

The thought pattern then forms an emotional response in the body, which gives us an awareness or insight into our subconscious relationship to the data. For example, if you see or hear something that you have learned is positive, you may experience a feeling that is good or pleasant. If you see or hear something that you have learned is negative, you may experience a feeling that is bad or unpleasant. It's important to understand that your relationship to the event you encounter may not be based in truth. Many of the things we learn throughout life are based on the false perceptions and misunderstandings of others. When this is the case, what you feel may not be an accurate indicator of the reality of the event, which is essential to know and understand if you want to change your experience with it.

Sometimes it is difficult to know what thoughts you are having, as they can be outside your conscious awareness at any given time. I have created processes to help you identify and change them, which you will learn in the upcoming chapters. The main point to remember here is that anytime you are feeling emotions that you don't like or want, it is only a product of the thought patterns that have come from the subconscious relationships and associations to the data or events outside of you. In other words, you are only feeling your thoughts, not the event. Let's try an exercise to demonstrate this point. Sit with your back straight, shoulders back, and your head facing forward. Close your eyes, think of a happy thought or memory, and smile as big as you can for thirty seconds. While continuing to sit straight up with a smile on your face, open your eyes and take notice of how good you feel. This is your emotional state responding to your thought pattern.

Your emotional state then drives your actions and behaviors, which lead to the experiential outcomes you produce. This cycle reinforces itself, causing you to continue doing the same things or creating the same results for yourself. To change this, you must address the thought processes. You will have to work with the thought processes rather than the subconscious filter because that's where your conscious experience begins and you don't have direct access to your subconscious mind. We want to make sure we are working to reach the subconscious mind effectively rather than just the process of experience it produces. To do this, you will need to create a new filtration system that can serve as a replacement to the one that is currently in place in the subconscious mind.

It's vitally important to understand that what I'm talking about has nothing to do with diverting your attention from the negative thoughts that are producing negative feelings by replacing them with positive thoughts. Ignoring negative thoughts because they don't feel good is not the answer to your healing. For several years now, a massive positive thought movement has been teaching people to discard negative thoughts that cause them pain and replace them with better-feeling thoughts. This is not a practical approach and rarely ever works long term to help people. The negative recurring thought patterns are an indicator of conflict. Pushing them aside to feel better only buries the conflict. By doing this, you will set yourself up for more considerable pain and conflict in the future. The effective way to handle this is to address the thought patterns directly. You must have the courage to face these negative thoughts and the pain they create if you want to resolve them for good. Remember, the pain has a purpose and you no longer have to run from it. You can take steps to resolve it so it never comes up again.

This is where responsibility comes into play. You are responsible for your experiences. Anytime you feel bad or have negative emotions, you must take responsibility by addressing the thought patterns creating them. It may seem like someone outside of you is responsible and should be held accountable, but the truth is that they cannot control your experiences. If they could, they would have your power. You are the only one who has that power to change and recreate your experiences in life. It is your job, nobody else's. This is important to accept and embrace. This gives you the power to change the things that aren't serving you the way you want in your life. Sure, you may be caught up in a situation or circumstance that you can't get out of, at least at this moment. But how you experience that situation or circumstance can be altered through taking responsibility and holding yourself accountable for your thoughts and emotions. Don't be too hard on yourself. Holding yourself accountable does not mean beating yourself up, scolding yourself, or even disciplining yourself for doing things in a way that doesn't serve you. It means that you acknowledge where the problem is, why it's there, and how you can change it from that point forward. Always be kind and loving toward yourself, no matter what.

Becoming aware of your emotions as much as possible is the key to taking responsibility. Like many of the other processes I talk about in this book, this is a mental muscle that you must exercise to grow. Awareness is said to be the key to life. When you become aware of something, you have the power to respond rather than react. Most people aren't aware of their thought patterns, so they react rather than respond to them because that's what they've always done or learned to do. When you become more aware of your thought patterns, you can consciously choose your response rather than allowing your emotions to drive ineffective actions that can have devastating consequences. When you become aware that you're not feeling good emotionally, you must jump into action. This is how you begin taking responsibility.

The first step to doing this is by asking yourself this question: "What is the truth?" Remember, the truth has nothing to do with your feelings, so when you ask this question, do so without regard to them. I had a client once who was frustrated at his wife for planting her flowers in a specific place in the yard. He made a compelling argument of how it would disrupt his usual way of mowing and tending to the yard work. When I asked him if he wanted his wife to plant the flowers there, he responded emphatically with, "No!" After talking with him further about his marriage and what he truly wanted for himself and his wife, he concluded that he did want her to plant the flowers there. The truth was that he wanted his wife to be able to express herself the way she wanted. He wanted to cocreate with her. He wanted her to be happy and do the things in life she wanted to do, and he wanted to be part of those things with her and to support her happiness. Planting the flowers in the yard allowed him to achieve this goal with her. The problem was not the flowers but rather the idea of inconvenience it would cause him. Once he saw this from a higher level of thinking, he was more than happy to make the adjustments necessary to accommodate her flowers.

An old saying from a Spider-Man comic book says, "With great power comes great responsibility." I have learned in my years that the more responsibility you take, the more power you gain. When you take responsibility in negative emotional states and address the thought patterns that created them, you can find relief—not just temporary relief but permanent relief as well. This can allow you to begin resolving the conflicts in the subconscious programs by breaking the cycle and creating new responses to the data. It isn't always easy to get yourself to take responsibility for your emotional state. Things happen externally that will cause you to justify your emotions. When something bad happens and we feel bad, we feel justified in our emotions. Sometimes when we feel bad, something inside us wants to stay there by listening to a sad song or doing something that allows those feelings to linger. We feel drained or unmotivated to pull ourselves out of that negative emotional state. This is normal and happens because our programs are designed to ensure we stay in those emotional states to reinforce them.

Remember, subconscious programs don't like to change. It goes against their nature. This is when discernment must come into play. Though you may feel like staying in that emotional state at that time, the truth is that you don't want to. It doesn't feel good, and it's not where you want to be, so you must exercise your strength at those moments and address the thought patterns. This is where the new filtration system of truth comes into play. Through this new filtration system of truth, you will discover that most of the conflicts you are experiencing are primarily based on lies and distortions of reality.

# CHAPTER 10

# SELF-MANAGEMENT

As we begin to delve into the tools and techniques I have designed to help you address the issues you experience in life that are causing anxiety and depression, there are a few understandings that are important to know and remember. Everything follows the law of process. Understanding how to use the tools I will teach you in this book will take some time to get used to and fluent with. Think of it like a muscle. The more you use it and exercise it, the stronger it grows. Don't expect to get it right the first or even the second time. Be patient with yourself and know there is a learning curve you will have to go through. With practice, you will become proficient and able to use them with greater ease and effectiveness. Practice, practice, practice! That's the key.

You may not feel like using them when you are in a disempowered state of feeling bad or negative, but when you do, you will find great relief and growth. For many years, I found myself going in circles and recreating the same destructive patterns and experiences in my life. I always seemed to end up in the same state of disempowerment and emptiness. When I developed these tools and noticed the profound changes they created, I decided to use them anytime I was struggling. That decision has made me happy, successful, and free from those old cycles in my life for good. It wasn't always easy or convenient, but I was determined and committed, and you must be as well.

The concepts behind these tools are simple, but using them may not be easy at first. With practice, you will be able to use them at any time for any reason. Do not be discouraged or overwhelmed at the length or depth of the breakdown of these tools as you go through them. They are broken down in a lengthy format to explain how to use them fully. When you use them on your own, you will find the process is much shorter and more feasible than it may appear in this book. However, I do encourage you at first to use the breakdown processes as I teach them to you so you can develop a deeper understanding, which will allow you to become more proficient and effective with them. But this is not necessary once you fully understand them.

## Needs versus Wants

Sometimes even just a slight change in how we view or think about things can make a significant difference in how we experience them. One of those things that can create a substantial difference in your life is when you begin differentiating between your needs and your wants. You only have four basic needs: food, shelter, water, and clothing. Outside of those four things are only desires. So many people walk around saying they need this or that to have this or that. We've been conditioned to think this way, but that type of thinking can hold you down and even reinforce the program that you're not enough. Every time you say or think that you need something outside of your basic needs, you come from a place of lack or not enough. When we think from a disempowered state, we create disempowered results in our lives. When we think from a place of desire, we come from a place of empowerment and expansion. Anything you want to create or experience in your life outside of your four basic needs is a desire, not a necessity. Here are a few common examples to illustrate this point:

**Disempowered thought: I need to lose weight.**
**Empowered thought: I would like to release thirty pounds.**

**Disempowered thought: I need more money.**
**Empowered thought: I would like to increase my income by four hundred dollars each month.**

**Disempowered thought: I should take better care of myself.**
**Empowered thought: I would like to take better care of my body by**
**exercising and eating healthy.**

Becoming more aware of how you speak and think about things will change your life significantly when you begin to filter them through a more empowering process. When we think from a place of need and lack, we are sending out signals that we are not or do not have enough of whatever it is we want. This creates more of these same thought patterns, and we become limited by them. When we think from an empowered place of expansion, we begin to see new possibilities and opportunities from outside of ourselves.

What you put out through the mental field will determine what you receive in the emotional and physical fields. It can create a sense of excitement when we begin to think this way because we are made and desire to create more and this is an optimum state of creating. We all love to do what we want to do, so when we step into an empowering thought process, we can see that we want and desire to create these new experiences and things in our lives to become more than we are currently being. This can fuel new passions and motivations behind our desires, which will initiate the reticular activating system in the brain to help us create them. Thinking from a place of need and lack will only create more need and lack in your life. Be mindful of your thoughts and how you speak about things. Change the disempowered thoughts to empowered thoughts and begin to see how it shifts your reality and improves your experience.

## Discernment and Self-Regulation

One of the most important things you will need to learn to do to overcome anxiety and depression, or to better your life in almost any way, is to self-regulate. Self-regulation is the ability to manage your emotional states effectively, which happens by regulating your thought patterns since emotions are a response to them. When you don't feel good emotionally, there is a conflict in your thought patterns. Since thought patterns come from the subconscious programs and belief systems, and we can't go to the subconscious mind directly to resolve the conflict without the use of tools such as hypnotherapy, we must correct the thought patterns in the conscious mind. This is where discernment comes into play. Discernment is the ability to judge something well or effectively. To achieve this, we must have a standard of measurement to judge things by—or what I like to call a filter. Truth is the most effective standard of measurement to filter or process thoughts that I have ever learned or worked with because it is universal and doesn't change based on situations or circumstances.

Think of discernment as a muscle. The more you use it and work it out, the stronger it becomes. As you work through these processes, you will begin to discover that most of your emotional pain comes from lies you have accepted in the subconscious mind. When our thoughts are aligned with truth, we typically don't feel pain in the emotional state. Truth has a powerful way of eliminating negative feelings by either neutralizing them completely or changing them into positive feelings such as relief, joy, and freedom. To effectively begin discerning between truth and lies in this way, we must bring a new level of awareness to our feelings and thoughts as well as understand that our feelings are not always aligned with our true desires.

You can achieve this by taking time to ask yourself as much as possible throughout the day questions such as "What is the truth in this situation?" or "Is this what I truly want and desire to do or is it just how I feel at this moment?" When you do this, you will notice that most of the things you do are based on your feelings and emotions, not your true desires. Feelings and emotions are nothing more than the body's response to a thought, and your thoughts are not always rooted in truth. When your true desires and feelings are not in alignment, using the power of discernment and acting based on your true desires, the feelings will typically line up with those thought patterns so you can make decisions that are more effective.

I want you to do what you want to do in life, but you will not always feel like doing it. There can be a big difference between what you want to do and what you feel like doing. As I began to understand this in my life and discovered that I was basing my actions on how I felt rather than what I truly desired, which robbed me of the things I truly wanted to do, I made a decision that I was going to do the things I truly wanted to do even if I didn't feel like it. This has served me more than I could begin to tell you. There are still times that I take action based on the feelings I am experiencing at the expense of my true desires, but when this happens, I try to do it consciously while taking full responsibility for my choices. When you give in to your feelings, they will generate more of those same feelings. When you recognize your true desires, your feelings will align with those thoughts and help you step into truth and guide your actions toward them.

I'll share an example from my own life to illustrate this practice and understanding. I was walking through the grocery store and came upon a display of Krispy Kreme Doughnuts. Anyone who knows me knows that I love Krispy Kreme glazed doughnuts. I walked up to this display thinking, *I think I'd like to buy a box of these doughnuts!* Then I paused for a moment to ask myself some crucial questions: *Is that the truth? Do I really want to buy this box of doughnuts or do I just feel like buying them?* Typically, when my wife or I buy a box of doughnuts, I eat up to five or six in a row. They're just so good! I thought about this scenario of how I would be tempted to eat too many doughnuts, which I most likely would. Then I would feel nasty inside and carry around the regret and guilt of doing so because I didn't stick to my plan of trying to eat somewhat healthy and take care of my body the way I wanted to.

Once that passed, I would still be left with more doughnuts and may be tempted to do the very same thing to myself again. This scenario has taken place many times over in my life, and I decided I didn't want to experience it anymore. Once I stepped into the truth of my desires that I didn't want to buy a box of doughnuts, I just continued my shopping without it. I understood that it wasn't just a box of doughnuts I was contemplating on buying. It was an experience. By taking the time to gain an awareness of the experience I would create if I bought the doughnuts and my true desire to eat more healthily and take care of my body, I was able to recognize the truth and make a choice that served me well. Afterward, I chuckled when I became aware that I'd lied to myself by thinking I wanted that box of doughnuts.

Without practicing discernment, I would have bought that experience and allowed myself to believe and act on a lie. This may seem like a silly little scenario, but when we begin to recognize that it's not always the big things that hold us back in life but instead the many small things that become a significant source of pain or suffering, we begin to understand that taking care of the little things is vital to our mental, emotional, spiritual, and physical health.

Let's go through a few examples from some clients I have worked with to implement a new level of awareness and discernment in their lives to create higher levels of self-regulation, happiness, and effective decisions. There are different ways of implementing the process of discernment to uncover the lies and the truth. I will teach you the methods I use to help others and myself. The main thing to remember is that the process of discernment is all about bringing awareness to the thoughts or emotions and then questioning them to ensure they are in-line with the truth. If they aren't, align them with truth so you can make more effective decisions that serve your highest good. The first and last step will be the same for each of the three discernment processes. Steps two and three may change based on which process you are using.

## Discernment Process I

## Effective Decision Making

This first process of discernment is the most common one I use for myself and others when dealing with the struggles of making a good decision as it relates to actions and behaviors.

**Example I:** First I will break down my situation with the Krispy Kreme doughnuts.

**Step I:** The first step is to become aware of and identify the thoughts and feelings you are experiencing at the moment.

*What thoughts and feelings are you experiencing?*

- **I would like to buy a box of Krispy Kreme doughnuts.**

**Step II:** Now it's time to become aware of the experiences you are or will create by accepting and acting on that thought or feeling.

*What results will you experience from buying a box of Krispy Kreme doughnuts?*

- **I'll probably get home and eat five or six of them in a row.**
- **I'll feel nasty inside from all that sugar.**
- **I'll feel guilty and ashamed that I didn't pace and take care of myself the way I really want and have been trying to.**
- **I'll beat myself up for giving in and not using better judgment for myself.**
- **I may gain some weight.**
- **I may do it all a second time since there will be several doughnuts left.**
- **I'll regret my decision and wish I hadn't bought the doughnuts in the first place.**

**Step III:** Now replace the words in the original statement with the experience it will or has created for you in the past and ask yourself if you truly desire that experience.

*Do you really want to buy the experience of getting home to eat five or six doughnuts in a row, which will make you feel nasty inside, guilty and ashamed for not taking care of yourself the way you have been trying to, causing you to beat yourself up, possibly gaining unwanted weight, and regretting your decision to buy the doughnuts with the possibility of doing it all again a second time?* **No.**

**Step IV:** Now it's time to recognize the truth versus the lie.

*What is the truth?* **The truth is, I don't want that experience at all. I've had it too many times to know that it will not nor has it ever served me well. I want to take care of myself and make healthy choices that keep me fit and feeling good physically. I don't want to walk around feeling that way about myself because it's destructive. I have goals that I want to reach and maintain, and I cannot achieve them by taking this action. I deserve to be treated better than that, so I will treat myself better. The truth is, I do not want to buy this box of doughnuts. It's just a feeling.**

Once I went through this process and aligned my thoughts and emotions with truth, I realized it was a lie and I didn't buy into it. It doesn't even come up for me when I see a display of doughnuts anymore because I could never buy into that lie again. I am more self-disciplined and successful at maintaining a healthier lifestyle and reaching my goals now.

**Example II:** This example comes from a client who wanted to lose weight but couldn't seem to get herself to follow through with an exercise routine. She was experiencing depression and anxiety in her life as well, which slowed her down and caused her to stay in her house and seclude herself. When I asked her why she felt she hasn't followed through with her desire to exercise and get out of the house more, she made the statement below.

**Step I:** *What thoughts and feelings are you experiencing?*

- **It's easier just to lie down and read than to exercise or go anywhere.**

**Step II:** *What results are you experiencing from not exercising or going out?*

- **I don't feel well.**
- **I continue to gain weight.**

- I don't socialize.
- My health has declined and continues to do so.
- I get even more depressed.
- My anxiety intensifies.
- I feel guilty and ashamed.
- I criticize and belittle myself.

**Step III:** *Is it "easier" to experience not feeling well, continuing to gain weight, not socializing, having your health decline, going through depression and anxiety, feeling guilty and ashamed, criticizing and belittling yourself rather than exercising or going anywhere?* **No.**

**Step IV:** *What is the truth?* **The truth is, it's harder to carry that stuff around all the time. It makes my life very difficult and unsatisfying. Sometimes I feel like it would be easier, and it may be in the moment, but in a bigger picture, it is much harder. It would be much easier to take a little time out of each day to get up and take care of myself, and I would feel much better by doing so. That's what I want to do.**

This client learned that she had been lying to herself without realizing it and was then taking actions based on that lie. Now, when that or similar thoughts come to her, she recognizes that it's a lie and she has a choice whether to take actions based on her true desires or her feelings. As a result, she stepped into an exercise routine that she stayed committed to and began to go out and enjoy her life more.

## Discernment Process II

## "Should" Statements, Guilt, and Shame

The second process of discernment is what I use when helping myself or others who are struggling with "should" thoughts and feelings that produce a variety of struggles, such as guilt, shame, and other disempowering thought patterns and emotional states. When we make "should" statements, we are seeing a standard or expectation we are putting on ourselves. Sometimes we believe it is us trying to meet someone else's standards or expectations, but in truth it is a standard or expectation that we have placed on ourselves—that we must meet someone else's standards or expectations. Or we are placing expectations upon ourselves that are unrealistic. Remember, everything eventually comes back to the self, even when we may not see or understand how at first.

**Example I:** This example comes from a woman who struggled with breaking the toxic emotional ties to her mother, who had narcissistic tendencies and was abusive toward her throughout her life. When people grow up in homes where they are exposed or subjected to abuse and neglect, they often form unhealthy or dysfunctional emotional ties to their abusers. In this case, she was trying to create healthy boundaries with her mother in a way that allowed her to maintain somewhat of a relationship with her without the abuse. She was experiencing this struggle with guilt after a holiday when she decided to go no contact with her mother so she could focus on herself and her family.

**Step I:**    *What thoughts and feelings are you experiencing?*

- **I should have called my mother. I feel guilty for not calling her.**
- **I should have done more than just send her flowers. I feel guilty for not doing more.**

**Step II:**   Now we break down the statements to understand the expectations we have placed on ourselves and the beliefs or programs within driving the thought patterns and emotional states. We do this by asking probing questions such as "Why?" or "Should you?" The more you break down each statement and answer you come up with the more effective this process can be for you.

*Why "should" you have called your mother?* **It is my duty to call my mom.** *Why "should" you have done more than just send her flowers?* **I am obligated to do more.**

**Step III:** The next step is to reveal any lies or inconsistencies from step II.

*Is it your "duty" to call your mom?* **No.**
*Are you "obligated" to do more than send her flowers?* **No.**

**Step IV:** *What is the truth?* **The truth is that I am not obligated to do anything at all, nor is it my duty to call her. My first obligation is to take care of my family and myself. By not calling her, I was doing that. I don't owe my mother anything at all, but I do owe it to myself to take care of me in the best way I can. I felt guilty because she always made me feel like it was my job, but she doesn't reciprocate, and that's not okay for me anymore. I feel good about my decision now because I know it was right for me and that I didn't do anything wrong.**

This client learned that she had been carrying around the idea that she was supposed to do all the work in her relationship with her mother. Throughout her life, when she didn't do what her mother wanted or thought was right for her, she would make her feel guilty, as if she had done something wrong, or punish her in some way. Being under this type of abuse caused her to take on a pattern of abuse and punish herself when she thought her mother disapproved of her or her actions. Once she had this realization, she was able to release the guilt associated with the belief system that she was supposed to please her mother, and she began taking better care of herself by doing what she believed was right for her and her family. This realization also helped her establish solid boundaries with her mother and stick to them.

**Example II:** This example comes from a young man who was struggling with where he was in his life. He was thirty-one years old, still single, and didn't have a house yet. He wanted all these things but judged himself for not having them yet. He would talk about how his friends had all these things by this point in their lives and felt that maybe something was wrong with him for not being where he was "supposed" to be.

**Step I:** *What thoughts and feelings are you experiencing?*

- **I should be so much further in life than where I am. I feel like a failure.**

**Step II:** *Why "should" you be somewhere or have something different than where you are and what you have in your life at this point?* **Because everyone else around me has these things already.**

*Does "everyone" that you know or have known who is thirty-one years old have these things?* **No.**

*Is there something wrong with what they have and where they are in life?* **No.**

*Does that mean they are failures for having what they have and being where they are in life?* **No.**

*If there are other guys your age that don't have these things and you believe that's okay, then what makes you different or for it not to be okay for you as well?* **Nothing.**

**Step III:** *"Should" you be further in life than where you are?* **I want to be, but that doesn't mean I "should" be.**

**Step IV:** *What is the truth?* **The truth is, I would like to have these things someday, but I'm okay where I am. Being where I am in life isn't that bad. To be honest, I don't feel ready or want to have those responsibilities in my life right now. I do what I want and how I want most of the time, and I like it that way. I'm comparing myself to others, but the truth is, I don't want what they want, nor do I want to be like them. I am on my journey, and that's okay for me.**

This client learned that he was holding himself to others' expectations and comparing himself to them and their ideas. He recognized that he was living his life the way he wanted and that where he was and what he had was right for him. He was able to let go of this expectation he placed on himself and enjoy his life as he had created it. He reported that after going through this process, when others made comments to him about his situation, he was able to stand in his power and confidently say that he was happy with his life the way it was and that maybe one day he would work toward those goals and that lifestyle, but not right then.

Over the years, as I have worked with many people to become free and empowered, I have found that so many issues they face come from placing unrealistic expectations on themselves based on what other people think they should be or do. By trying to please other people in this way, we tend to lose our own identity or, in some cases, never form one at all based on who we are and the values we hold. Authenticity is an essential part of being successful, happy, and free in life, and the only way we can achieve this is by doing what we feel is right for ourselves.

## Discernment Process III

## Identifying with Problems

The third process of discernment is what I use when helping myself or others who are struggling with identifying themselves with their situations or circumstances in life, causing them to feel and experience unnecessary emotional pain or dysfunctional patterns. When we disconnect our identity from our challenges, we can more efficiently and effectively begin to experience relief and make more significant progress in our lives.

**Example I:** This example comes from a young woman I worked with who struggled with her weight. She was distraught when she came in for her appointment after stepping onto the scale earlier that morning.

**Step I:**   *What thoughts and feelings are you experiencing?*

- I've gained too much weight.
- I can't believe I've let myself get into this situation.
- I'm unhealthy, overwhelmed, and it's depressing.

**Step II:**  This step is where we ask, "What does this mean or say about you?" to gain an understanding of how you may be identifying with your situation or circumstance.

*What does this mean or say about you?*

- I'm out of control.
- There's nothing I can do about it.
- I've wasted so much time that I could have taken to be and stay healthy.
- I'm lazy.

**Step III:**  Refer to step three in Discernment Process II.

*Are you really "out of control"?* **No.**

*Is there "nothing" you can do about your weight?* **Yes. I can exercise and eat healthily.**

*Have you "wasted" your time?* **No. I haven't taken the time to focus on staying healthy, but that doesn't mean I've wasted the time I had. I just used it on other things.**

*Are you a lazy person?* **No. I'm a very busy person, and I do a lot of things. I rarely even get a chance to be lazy.**

**Step IV:** *What is the truth?* **The truth is, I'm not out of control. I did let my focus shift away from my health and routine of maintaining my weight over the past few years, but I can turn that around at any time I choose. I went through some difficult times in life for a while and decided to let myself stop being active and eating healthily, but now I can adjust my focus and lose the weight. I can do this.**

This client learned that she had been identifying herself with her feelings and results. This caused her to feel negatively toward herself and punish herself through self-abuse. Those thoughts made her feel depressed and lowered her motivation, drive, and self-esteem. Now that she has worked out the lies and replaced them with truth, she feels empowered and has a routine she is consistent with. She has also replaced the self-judgment with self-love and is enjoying the process of recreating her physical appearance and health.

**Example II:** This example comes from an older gentleman who was experiencing some medical challenges that limited some of his physical capabilities. He expressed how his wife was doing the yard work and that he didn't like her having to pick up his typical duties.

**Step I:** *What thoughts and feelings are you experiencing?*

- **I feel like a burden to my wife.**
- **She shouldn't have to be outside, struggling to do what I'm supposed to be doing.**
- **I should be out there doing my part or at least helping her.**
- **I feel so useless.**

**Step II:** *What does this mean or say about you?*

- **I'm worthless.**
- **I'm no good to anybody.**
- **I'm a burden.**
- **I don't deserve to have her in my life.**

**Step III:** *Are you really "worthless" just because you can't help your wife in the yard right now?* **No. That doesn't mean anything about my value.**

*Are you really "no good" to anybody just because you can't physically do some things right now?* **No. I can still do helpful things.**

*Are you really a "burden" just because of your physical limitations right now?* **No. I feel like a burden because of the added duties she has taken on since I started having these problems, but that doesn't make me a burden.**

*Do you not deserve to have her in your life just because you are having some medical issues?* **I still deserve to have her in my life. I wish I could do more to help her right now. I love her, and I want to be there and do for her more than what I am physically capable of right now, but I still deserve to have her in my life, regardless of my limitations.**

**Step IV:** *What is the truth?* **The truth is, as I am going through this challenging time medically, my wife has to do some of the things I used to do and can't do right now. There's nothing wrong with her doing these things, and she says she is okay with doing them. I know it puts more pressure on her than I want, but that's what a husband and wife do for each other. There have been times in the past that I had to help more than usual, and I was okay with that because I love her. It's the same for her. The truth is, though it isn't my preference for her to do this work outside, it is okay, and I am very grateful to have her.**

This client learned that he was judging and condemning himself because he was struggling physically. When he became aware of the lies, he was able to turn his feelings of worthlessness into feelings of gratitude toward his wife. This was reciprocated from her and even made her feel better about doing the yard work. He recognized that his physical limitations did not define him as a person and had nothing to do with his value. Once he released feeling like a burden to his wife over his condition, he found new ways to become helpful and useful inside the house that didn't require a lot of physical effort. He now feels useful and grateful instead of useless and worthless.

## Putting Discernment into Practice

Practicing these processes of discernment will help you let go of destructive thought patterns, bring stability to your emotional state, heal the damaged parts of yourself, and take effective actions that will move you from where you are to where you want to be in life. It will also help you begin to understand what truth is and how to use it in your life more effectively. It's not always necessary to write out the thoughts or emotions you are experiencing to change them, but it is a useful practice that I encourage because when you write them out, you can view them objectively and get rid of them entirely in most cases. When you hold things inside of your mind, they remain subjective, or part of you. By writing them out, you can approach them objectively, and in most cases, see them for what they are and are not.

Many of the examples are dealing with situations and circumstances that may not seem to have much to do with anxiety or depression, but each of these examples came from clients who suffered from either or both. As I stated previously, it's not always the big things that cause us anxiety or depression but instead the small things that accumulate over time and become overwhelming. Using the process of discernment with each thought or emotion that causes you discomfort, or before each decision you make regularly, will help you to train your mind to see truth more readily and will resolve many of the issues you may face that are adding to the anxiety or depression you experience. It can help you make more effective decisions and do what you want and desire in life that your emotions and feelings rob you of. When you align your thoughts with truth, you will experience greater freedom, happiness, security, and joy in your life.

# CHAPTER 11

# RESOLVING PROBLEMS

As you begin to align your thinking with truth based on the Model of Power and learn how your experiences are created through the Model of Human Experience, you will start thinking on a higher level to process your thoughts and emotions for more effective and desirable outcomes. You learned through the Model of Human Experience that all experiences you have, have had, or will have are not based on the events outside of yourself but rather your internal associations and relationships to them. Problems are not an exception to this. What you perceive as problems are only problems based on the way you are thinking about them. Anytime you have a problem that lingers or you can't seem to get around it, you feel stuck or disempowered. When you come to a new understanding of the problem you perceive, you gain a new insight or perception of it and can then have a new experience with it.

I made a bold statement that the emotional pain you experience in your life is primarily based on lies and distortions of truth, so let's explore this concept deeper. One of the primary tools I use for breaking down problems and conflict is a process I call PTIR: problem, truth, insight, responsibility. This process is designed to lay out a problem and all its effects, break down each statement through an evaluation of truth, define the truth about the problem, gain a deeper understanding of the driving factors behind it, and then decide what steps of responsibility you can take to change it based on the truth and insight of your experience.

Here's the catch to using this tool: you *must* write it down for it to work to the degree of effectiveness required to reach the root of the problems and resolve them. The mind cannot effectively process at one time all the information coming out in this process. Doing this in your head will render only mediocre results by helping you feel better emotionally in the moment, but it typically will not resolve the problems in the end. This means that they will continue to reoccur throughout your life. Let's go through the breakdown of the PTIR process for resolving the conflicts and problems in your life.

**Example I:** Let's begin with an example a former client needed help resolving. She said that she trusted people too easily, which caused her to get her feelings hurt because they always ended up using her. This led to her building emotional walls that blocked anyone from getting too close, which left her feeling alone. She said that she didn't want to build new friendships because they didn't work out for her, so she decided to stop trying to make new friends. Let's look at the process of PTIR that I used to help her resolve this conflict and move toward a more desirable experience and outcome.

## Part I: Problem

Step 1:   State the problem in a short, concise statement:

*What is the problem?*               **I trust people too easily.**

Step 2:   Once you have stated the problem, begin to write down why this is a problem for you in your life. For each answer you come up with, ask why that is or what makes it a problem in life for you. This is not the time to psychoanalyze the deeper meaning of why you're experiencing the problems but instead the surface issues based on your feelings or conscious perception. You may only come up with a few statements or many in this step of the process. The number of statements is not important but instead making sure you complete this step fully to ensure you get down to the root of the problem.

*Why is/what makes this a problem?*    **I find out they always end up using me.**

*Why is/what makes this a problem?*    **I get my feelings hurt.**

*Why is/what makes this a problem?*    **It makes me feel stupid.**

*Why is/what makes this a problem?*    **I beat myself up because I should've seen it coming.**

*Why is/what makes this a problem?*    **It drains my energy.**

*Why is/what makes this a problem?*    **It keeps me from being productive.**

*Why is/what makes this a problem?*    **I don't want to build new friendships with people.**

*Why is/what makes this a problem?*    **I feel empty and lonely.**

*Why is/what makes this a problem?*    **I'm stuck, being alone without anyone to share my life with.**

Step 3:    Now that you've asked why or what makes this a problem for you in your life and possibly reached the point where you've exhausted all thoughts, it's time to ask the deeper question of what this means or says about you as a person. Again, this is not the time to psychoanalyze your answers, thoughts, or feelings but rather just let the surface emotions and thoughts present themselves. You may not have any responses to this question, and it may not be applicable to every problem. If not, just skip this portion of the process.

*What does this mean about you?*    **I don't deserve to have friends.**

*What does this mean about you?*    **Nobody really cares about me.**

*What does this mean about you?*    **I'm no good.**

*What does this mean about you?*    **I'm worthless, and I should just give up.**

Step 4:    In step four, you will need to observe each of your statements objectively and without bias or emotions against the truth. This may seem difficult at first, but it is necessary to expose the lies you may have bought into so you can begin healing and overcoming this problem in your life. It's time to ask the question "Is this true?" for each statement. Discard any emotions or justifications and evaluate each statement solely on whether it is the truth. If you need a refresher on how to use truth as a filter, revisit the section on truth in chapter five. You will notice that some of these statements are based on feelings and emotions. When this is the case, we begin to ask further questions to ensure we gain objective clarity of the truth. I will identify these statements with an asterisk (*). So let's examine each of these statements against the filter of truth to see what's happening in this example.

*Problem statement:* **I trust people too easily.** *Is this statement true? Do you trust people "too easily"?* **No. I do trust people easily and quickly, but to say I trust them too easily would be a false statement because that would be implying I'm doing something wrong by trusting someone before I should or without enough of a reason. Trusting people is not a bad thing. I want to trust people.**

**I find out they always end up using me.** *Is this statement true? Do they "always" end up using you?* **No. Friends in the past have used me, but they don't "always" end up using me. I have had friends that haven't used me. In truth, I can't make a blanket statement like that.**

**I get my feelings hurt.** *Is this statement true? Do you get your feelings hurt?* **Yes. Sometimes I do get my feelings hurt by others, and it does hurt when I am being used.**

**\*It makes me feel stupid.** *Is this statement true? Do you feel stupid?* **Yes.** *Does being used by someone make you a stupid person?* **No. I'm very smart. Even though I feel this way, I realize that it's not true about me.**

**I beat myself up because I should've seen it coming.** *Is this statement true? "Should" you have seen it was coming?* **No. I guess there's no way I could have seen it coming and no reason I "should" have. I'm not perfect or psychic.**

*It drains my energy.* Is this statement true? Does "it" drain your energy? No. "It" doesn't drain my energy. The way I feel about it and how I respond to it is what drains my energy. "It" doesn't have power over me unless I give my power to it.

*It keeps me from being productive.* Is this statement true? Does "it" keep you from being productive? No. I keep myself from being productive; "it" doesn't.

*I don't want to build new friendships with people.* Is this statement true? Do you want to build new friendships with people? No. I do want to build new friendships with people. I enjoy having friends, and the truth is I miss having more of them. I have allowed the hurt of a few friendships that turned sour to become more important and significant to me than what I want.

*I feel empty and lonely.* Is this statement true? Do you feel empty and lonely? Yes. I feel as if I have so much to give and nobody to give it to. I understand that you feel empty and lonely, but are you empty or alone? No.

*I'm stuck, being alone without anyone to share my life with.* Is this statement true? Are you really "stuck" being alone? No. I'm not stuck being alone. There are many people in my life now and many more people I may have the opportunity to meet in the future.

*I don't deserve to have friends.* Is this statement true? Do you not deserve to have friends? No. I do deserve to have friends.

*Nobody really cares about me.* Is this statement true? Are you uncared for? No. I have a lot of people who care about me.

*I'm no good.* Is this statement true? Are you really a "no-good" person? No. I am a good person. I help people and try my best to be a good person in life.

**I'm worthless, and I should just give up.** *Is this statement true? Are you really without worth? Should you just give up?* **No. I do have worth, and I shouldn't just give up.**

# Part II: Truth

Part II of this process is all about gaining insight and proper perspective on the real problem and redefining it so it can be resolved. Once you have broken down the problem and have evaluated each statement through the filter of truth, it's time to take a step back and objectively observe your previous statements to discover and define the truths behind this problem. Let's see what this part of the process looks like by asking the following question:

*What is the truth?*

**The truth is, I am punishing myself by not building new friendships because of a few experiences that hurt my feelings, which have caused me to devalue and mistreat myself. Sometimes friendships end, but that's no reason for me not to have them.**

**The truth is, I do want to build friendships with others, and I can have healthy, fulfilling friendships in my life.**

**The truth is, I have mistreated myself and judged my value and worth based on someone else's actions, but the actions of others do not define my value and worth. I am worthy, and I do deserve to have good friends in my life.**

# Part III: Insight

This part of the process is where you can begin to gain insight into the belief systems or programs causing the thought processes creating pain or conflict in your life. To achieve this successfully, you must objectively observe each part of this process without regard to your emotions to see the truth about your experience and what within you created it. To recognize that you created this experience, typically in an unconscious way, can give you the awareness and ability to address and begin changing the core belief systems or programs that created them so you can successfully rewire your brain to produce a different response or result. This part of the process is usually reserved for those who have become fluent with this technique but can be used by the beginners who allow themselves to see past their surface perception and emotions. Now let's see what insight we can gain from this example.

We can see that she has a tendency, at least in this area of her life, to define her future based on her past. When we do this, we are most likely to reproduce those same results or experiences in our life repeatedly. We call these cycles, and most people experience them in many areas of their life.

We can see that she is punishing herself, which is equivalent to emotional abuse because it's causing her to suffer and develop dysfunctional behaviors and patterns in her life. Becoming aware of this allows her to replace the emotional abuse with self-love and compassion. If she had any friends who were going through this or a similar situation, she would likely show them love and compassion and do her best to comfort them. This pattern reveals a lack of self-love.

The value proposition shows up here in a big way as well. She has concluded that she doesn't have a lot of value based on the actions of others and used that as a confirmation, thus reinforcing a program of worthlessness. This led to her lack of self-love. Love is an action, not a feeling. It produces feelings, but love is experienced through action or interaction. It is common for people to take action based on their feelings, but when there is a lack of feelings of love toward oneself, only through taking action first to show themselves love will they then create and experience the feelings of love toward themselves.

When we see the value proposition in this way, it usually doesn't stem from the situation itself. This program or belief system is typically installed as a child and becomes a recurring pattern that is expressed in many ways throughout life. When this is the case, it often takes some time to reprogram that belief system, depending on how deep-rooted the program is. A rule of thumb I use based on my own experiences, and through the work I have done with others, is to reduce each year of the negative programming down to a month of healing. So if you have been living with this program for thirty years, it may take thirty months to reprogram this belief system fully. This doesn't mean that it will take thirty months to experience or receive results from your work, just that it may take that amount of time to fully reprogram that belief system because it's so entwined throughout many different areas of your life. Every step you take will begin to produce new results in your life so stick with it!

She also shows signs of not trusting her judgment and using an all-or-nothing mindset. Her statement "I find out they always end up using me" shows us that she believes she *always* uses poor judgment when it comes to letting people into her life. This reveals a program or belief system that says she is not smart or lacks intelligence in this area. When a person doesn't trust their judgment, they rely on the judgment of others or they shut everyone out completely to avoid any pain that may result from a bad decision. We can see that she has done this by withdrawing into herself and blocking out any new opportunities to form new healthy relationships. In other words, she causes herself the pain she now believes she deserves by depriving herself of what she truly desires instead of learning to improve her judgment skills when it comes to an understanding of what she wants and needs from a relationship with others and going after what she desires.

**Core factors to address: Value proposition, self-love, self-regulation**

## Part IV: Responsibility

Part IV is all about stepping back into your power by deciding what steps of responsibility you can take now with the insight you have gained through truth to resolve this problem for yourself. Let's observe what this part of the process looks like by asking the following question:

*What steps of responsibility can you take now based on the truths and insight you have learned?*

**The first step of responsibility I can take is to recognize my value and know I do deserve to and can have good friendships in my life. I can do this by deliberately acknowledging that I am valuable and worthy each day and taking the necessary time to take loving actions toward myself, such as reinforcing these truths throughout each day and night. I understand that having a healthy relationship with myself first is most important.**

**I can allow myself to release the past by recognizing that my future doesn't have to depend on or be decided by it. I can be open to new possibilities and opportunities for my life by staying present and loving myself.**

**I can allow myself to learn from my past mistakes by using them to help me identify what I want and need from a relationship with others. I can look for those qualities in myself first and then others to ensure I am stepping into a healthy relationship that will serve everyone well.**

**I can reach out to a few people I know I am compatible with who have tried to connect with me yet I rejected because of the walls I built around my emotions and heart. I can take my time to get to know them and allow them to get to know me to make sure they are healthy for me. If they are not healthy, I can lovingly release them while still loving myself.**

Because of this process, she was able to develop a healthy relationship and a more profound sense of love and compassion for herself. She realized that she needed to first go within and change the programs and belief systems that created these cycles in her life. Now she enjoys having healthy relationships with others and herself, which brings deeper meaning and fulfillment to her life. She understands the necessity of continuing to work on these programs within herself through daily reinforcement and mindfulness so she can sustain her new results and continue producing even greater results in these areas of her life in the future.

**Example II:** This next example comes from a young man who struggled with meeting others' expectations for him and how he should live his life. This caused him to form destructive and dysfunctional behaviors and patterns in his life that destabilized his emotions and relationships with others, including his own family.

## Part I: Problem

Step 1:   *What is the problem?*   **I fall short of others' expectations.**

Step 2:   *Why is/what makes this a problem?*   **It causes me to worry.**

*Why is/what makes this a problem?*   **It makes life more stressful.**

*Why is/what makes this a problem?*   **I can't enjoy life as much.**

*Why is/what makes this a problem?*   **It makes me angry and affects my mood.**

*Why is/what makes this a problem?*   **It affects other people and their lives.**

Step 3:   *What does this mean about you?*   **I don't know.**

*Note: Sometimes you will not have an answer to this question, and that is perfectly okay. Just move on to the next step.

Step 4:   *Is this statement true?*

Problem statement: **I fall short of others' expectations.** *Is this statement true? Do you fall short of others' expectations of you?* **No. Sometimes people put higher expectations on me that are unrealistic, so I guess in that regard I do, but not in a general sense.**

**It causes me to worry.** *Is this statement true? Does "it" cause you to worry?* **No. I let myself focus on the thoughts of what others think about me and apply that to my life as a judgment against myself because I can't meet their expectations of what I should be. I cause myself to worry by caring more about what they think than what I think is right for me.**

**It makes life more stressful.** *Is this statement true? Does "it" make life more stressful?* **No. I stress myself out by taking on those ideas and expectations of others that I know are not right for me. It's as if I set myself up for failure, which I then allow myself to become stressed out about.**

**I can't enjoy life as much.** *Is this statement true? Can you "not" enjoy life as much?* **No. How I enjoy my life and to the degree doesn't depend on other people, their expectations, or whether I am experiencing some stress or not. It depends on me and the way I choose to see things. I can choose to enjoy life more by letting things go and not caring about what others think about me. In that respect, I guess I can enjoy life more.**

**It makes me angry and affects my mood.** *Is this statement true? Does "it" make you angry or affect your mood?* **No. I guess I allow myself to get angry at my response of feeling stressed and then taking actions that don't end up serving me the way I want.**

**It affects other people and their lives.** *Is this statement true? Does "it" affect other people and their lives?* **No. It doesn't affect other people. I choose to take out my feelings on others by mistreating them. How I am reacting to my feelings is what affects other people's lives, not the feelings or situations themselves.**

## Part II: Truth

*After examining the above statements, what truths do you see?*

The truth is, I am holding myself to others' expectations. I don't always meet the expectations of others, and that's okay. The part I struggled with was my expectation that I had to please others or meet their expectations. When I didn't meet my expectations of meeting others' expectations, I would focus on that which caused me to become worried and stressed out. My focus on these negatives caused me not to live my life the way I wanted, which then turned into anger that I directed at other people I blamed for my experiences.

The truth is, my expectation that I needed to meet the expectations of others is entirely unrealistic for me.

The truth is, I haven't been taking responsibility for myself entirely by defining my expectations based on what I want and believe I am or could be and what is right for me.

## Part III: Insight

We can see that he has learned to judge himself based on the opinions and expectations of others. This didn't serve him well because he was unable to meet those standards, or perceived standards, of others, which caused him many struggles and lowered his perceived value and opinion of himself. When we see this type of thinking, we can see patterns of reverse projection. Reverse projection takes place when someone places their ideas or beliefs onto others as if the other person feels or thinks what they feel or think. When this happens, the person tends to form dysfunctional behaviors and patterns in their life, such as anxiety, depression, or in some cases, more severe mental disorders.

We can also see the value proposition at work in his life. People who try to satisfy others' expectations and ideas of who and how they should be in life are typically those who don't feel like they are enough on their own. They believe that if they can fit the mold of others or their environment, then they will be accepted, which will add to their value. This is never the case. Only by being authentic and standing in one's own power can they connect with their value and find their true place in this world.

Core factors to address: Value proposition, self-expectation

# Part IV: Responsibility

*What steps of responsibility can you take now based on the truths and insight you have learned?*

I can take the time to develop and define my expectations and standards for my life for who I am, who I want to be, and what I want for myself. I can examine my own beliefs and determine what is right for me without worrying about what other people think about it.

I can live based on the beliefs I feel are right for me and my life.

I can release my desire for approval from others by accepting myself more fully and minding my own business, which has nothing to do with what others think or feel about me.

I can begin to recognize my value and follow my heart. This will lead me to where I'm supposed to be in life, and wherever that is, I want to be there.

As a result of this process, he was able to focus on himself rather than others by creating standards for himself based on what he felt was right for himself. He no longer lives with the internal conflict in his mind of trying to meet the expectations of others and instead focuses on what he wants in life. He recognizes his value and takes time to nurture himself in healthy ways that have allowed him the freedom to be who he is and wants to be. In this, he found the happiness, freedom, and security to express himself authentically.

When you begin to work with the PTIR process, you may have difficulty defining the truth or understanding what the truth is in that situation or under the specific circumstances you are looking at. People often confuse facts with truth in this process. Facts are things that we have justified or proven to be true based on the conclusion of evidence we look at, but not all facts are universal truths. Universal truth will not waver or change based on the situation or circumstance. Truth has nothing to do with emotions or feelings either. To perform this technique effectively, you must put aside your feelings and be objective in your approach. Your emotions will justify and reinforce hanging on to the old ideas and ways of looking at things, whereas being objective with the truth will expose any false ideas or lies creating negative emotions. With practice, you will become proficient in discovering the truth in this way.

# CHAPTER 12

# OVERCOMING INTRUSIVE THOUGHTS

Some of the most common issues people experience come from intrusive thoughts. These are the negative or unwanted thoughts that pop into your mind, seemingly out of nowhere. Every person experiences intrusive thoughts, but sometimes they can feel overwhelming and cause great struggle and difficulty. You may experience these in the form of self-doubt, self-criticism, self-degrading, violence, and many other ways. Sometimes these thoughts can even be scary and troubling. Good people have negative intrusive thoughts as well, which can make them question whether they are good people, but we should understand that the thoughts in our minds do not dictate or determine whether we are good—or anything else, for that matter. They are only thoughts and only have the power we give to them.

These thoughts can often intensify depression or anxiety. As you learned earlier, depression and anxiety are caused by thought patterns that are based on the negatives of the past and future. If left unaddressed, they can also keep you there. It's important not to label or identify yourself with these thought patterns. They are common and do not mean anything about you. It's part of life and part of the step you are in. When the programs causing them are addressed, you will likely experience little to none of them. Either way, they are just thoughts and do not define you or have any power over what you do or who you are—unless you allow them to.

Now that you have learned some new skills through the discernment and PTIR process, it's time to use those skills of discovering the truth to begin dissolving your intrusive thoughts. As with the PTIR process, for this tool to be most effective, you must write it out. Using this process to address them when they arise can bring you great relief from suffering. One of the first things to understand when dealing with unwanted negative thoughts is how *not* to get rid of them. Your first inclination may be to resist or fight them. This is absolutely the wrong way to achieve this. You cannot push or force thoughts out of your mind.

Remember the green apple exercise you went through in the "Shifting Your Focus" section of chapter eight? When you try to push or force something out of your mind, you will make it stick. When you're trying to get rid of an intrusive thought pattern causing you a lot of emotional pain by pushing it out of your mind, you will intensify the emotions, which will give it more power. Remember, one of the ways the subconscious mind learns is through high emotionally charged experiences. Your negative thoughts are an indicator of subconscious conflicts. Removing them can only happen when the conflict causing them is resolved. That's what the ITI (intrusive thoughts, truth, insight) process you are about to learn is designed to help you achieve. Using it as often as possible will help you uncover the lies and deceptions that are the primary source of your emotional pain and help you on your path to recovery from anxiety and depression. Let's look at the ITI process and how it can be applied.

**Example I:** This first example comes from a client I worked with who was having some struggles with pursuing his business goals. He expressed a lot of doubt in his ability to reach his goals and experienced a mental battle, with a negative voice constantly telling him he couldn't do it or that he wasn't good enough.

**Step I:   Intrusive Thoughts and Feelings**

The first step is to write down all intrusive thoughts and feelings that come to you about the subject you are focusing on. You may have five, ten, twenty, or even more intrusive thoughts that come to your mind. Don't concern yourself with how many; just make sure you write them all down. This is where you dig deep and do your best to pull every one of them out and put them on paper. You must get them all out for this technique to be most effective. Allow yourself to do this without filtering your thoughts. This is not the time to psychoanalyze them or yourself but instead to get them all out of you and down on paper. Don't be frightened by thoughts that seem dark or disturbing. Many people try to hold back the disturbing or dark thoughts because they are afraid to face them or know that they have them, but if you want to get rid of them, you must address them. Some people think that if they acknowledge or express the darker thoughts that they will bring those things upon themselves or even be punished for having them. This is not true. This process is about getting them out of you so they no longer reside within. Holding them in is what will cause you to experience the effects of them. This process is about addressing and freeing yourself from them. Allow yourself to be vulnerable and completely open as you use this technique.

Write out *all* intrusive thoughts and feelings you are experiencing.

1. **Who am I kidding? I can't do this.**
2. **I'm not good enough to pull this off.**
3. **Nobody will buy what I'm selling.**
4. **I don't deserve to succeed because I haven't worked hard enough.**
5. **Who do I think I am?**
6. **I don't belong here.**
7. **I'm a con.**
8. **Nobody is going to believe what I say.**
9. **Maybe I should just give up.**
10. **Maybe I'm just not cut out for this.**

## Step II: Truth

Now that you've exhausted all intrusive thoughts and feelings spiraling through your mind, it's time to evaluate each of them against the truth and make truth statements for each.

1.  Who am I kidding? I can't do this. *Is this true? Can you* **not** *do this?* The truth is, I can do this. I can make this happen. If I couldn't do it, then I wouldn't have been doing it all this time. My goal is stretching me, but with enough effort and believing in myself, I can make this happen.

2.  I'm not good enough to pull this off. *Is this true? Are you not good enough to pull this off?* The truth is, I am good enough to pull this off. I am valuable, and I do deserve to reach my goals. Other people who are no better than me have done it and so can I.

3.  Nobody will buy what I'm selling. *Is this true? Will nobody buy what you're selling?* The truth is, I have sold many policies in the past. So I guess people will buy what I'm selling because they've done so before.

4.  I don't deserve to succeed because I haven't worked hard enough. *Is this true? Do you not deserve to succeed? Have you not worked hard?* The truth is, I have worked very hard to get where I am. Though I'm not as successful as I want to be yet, I am still successful. I'm supporting my family and doing well. If I didn't deserve to succeed, then I wouldn't be successful. I do deserve to be successful.

5.  Who do I think I am? *Who are you? What's the truth about you?* The truth is, I am a man who is doing my best to support my family. I am successful in doing that. I've reached some goals in the past, and I can achieve goals in the future as well. I am someone who works hard for the money I make, and I deserve to be happy and have the things I want in life.

6.  I don't belong here. *Is this true? Do you not belong here?* The truth is, I do belong here. I wouldn't be here if I didn't.

7.  I'm a con. *Is this true? Are you really a con?* The truth is, I'm not a con. Sometimes I feel as if I'm presenting myself as someone

I'm not, but the truth is, I am only acting professionally and doing what I need to do for my customers, myself, and my family. I'm not lying or manipulating people, which is what a con does. Therefore, I'm not a con.

8. **Nobody is going to believe what I say.** *Is this true? Is nobody going to believe what you say?* **The truth is, I've never really had a problem with people not believing me. People tend to believe what I say to them. I have sold many policies that required the customers to believe me.**

9. **Maybe I should just give up.** *Is this true? Should you just give up?* **The truth is, I have no reason to give up. I just felt discouraged and wanted to avoid feeling that way, but I shouldn't just give up. I should pursue my goals and keep moving forward.**

10. **Maybe I'm just not cut out for this.** *Is this true? Are you not cut out for this?* **The truth is, I've done very well in the past. If I weren't cut out for this, then I would not have been as successful as I have been. I can continue to grow and get better so that I can reach my goals. I enjoy my work, and I am cut out for this.**

## Step III: Insight

To get to the core of the problems causing these intrusive thoughts to occur, you must evaluate your intrusive thoughts to gain a deeper insight as to why they are there. This advanced step of this process can be very helpful in your journey of healing but is not necessary for resolving the intrusive thought patterns. Intrusive thoughts are like roots of a seed. Taking a more in-depth look at them from the perspective of trying to understand what they are telling you will often lead you to the seed that is causing them. This insight can give you the power to address the root cause of the intrusive thoughts so you can remove those seeds and begin to heal. Step III is where you evaluate each statement to understand the core beliefs pushing the intrusive thoughts.

1. Who am I kidding? I can't do this. In this statement, we can see self-doubt through the idea that achieving his goals is out of his reach or character. This is the value proposition at play. When we look deeper into this statement, we want to begin asking questions about who "I" am and why "I" can't achieve this.

2. I'm not good enough to pull this off. This statement is supportive of the first statement and reveals that this person does not feel worthy enough to achieve what they want to achieve. We recognize that this person has work to do on the core aspect of self-value.

3. Nobody will buy what I'm selling. This statement reflects his low self-value, which is expressed onto external factors. The way we feel about ourselves is usually reflected through our external circumstances and situations. Many people tend to use this type of reflection to justify their position, which gives them permission or reason to hold on to that belief system by saying things like, "If I deserved it, then I would get it. I'm not getting it, so that must mean I don't deserve it." Be careful of this trap. Your external circumstances only reflect your belief systems currently in place. When you change the belief systems holding your current circumstances in place, you will receive reinforcement for the new ones through your external circumstances.

4. I don't deserve to succeed because I haven't worked hard enough. This reveals a belief system that value comes from how hard a person works. This is common in our society today because so much of our lives are spent judging or being judged by what we do. When someone works hard or achieves, they are rewarded. When they don't, either they don't get the rewards that someone who worked hard did or they are punished in some way. This system begins at a very young age and is foundational to learning what is right and wrong.

However, if not learned or applied in a healthy way, a child can grow up believing that they must work for their value. Many problems with this type of thinking cause various issues because it simply isn't the truth. A person's value has nothing to do with what they do, have done, or will do in their life. You can add value to others and this world through your actions; however, that doesn't increase your value as a person. If this were the case, people who do nothing would have no or low value, such as babies, sick people, or even elders who can no longer perform regular duties.

5. Who do I think I am? This statement speaks to the worthiness and value this person believes about themselves. It implies that he is not worthy or deserving of having and achieving his goals. Again, we see the value proposition at play here.

6. I don't belong here. This statement reveals a belief that this person feels that he is somehow less than adequate or unworthy of being in this position and that it's reserved for someone more deserving or better than he is. This shows a lack of confidence in his abilities and leads back to the value proposition.

7. I'm a con. This statement shows a distorted perception in this person's mind that reveals a belief that he is incapable of being worthy and good or trustworthy, at least in this capacity. His lack of confidence in himself and his abilities has created thought patterns that reinforce that he is either not a good person or not worthy of being in the position he is in.

8. Nobody is going to believe what I say. This statement shows a negative belief about himself and his credibility. Again, we see the value proposition at play here. His thoughts portray him as someone who doesn't look like a person who is worthy or trustworthy of someone else's business or that he is somehow not a good person and that others will perceive him as such.

He places this projection of himself on others as if they view him the same way he perceives himself. This type of belief system can come from an upbringing in which the caretakers didn't display a healthy level of trust or confidence in their child.

9.  Maybe I should just give up. This statement reveals the defense mechanism of this person to escape this situation. This is usually due to a person not having healthy coping skills to handle or resolve issues so they escape them by withdrawing or avoiding dealing with the underlying problems taking place. The purpose of this defense mechanism is to keep the person safe by keeping them out of a situation that may bring them harm or pain. The harm or pain doesn't have to be real for the subconscious mind to perceive it as such. This also shows a trace of the value proposition at play that says that he doesn't deserve to have the things he truly desires. This program is trying to survive through self-sabotaging thoughts and behaviors.

10. Maybe I'm just not cut out for this. Along with traces of the value proposition we see in this statement is the defense mechanism of escaping. Now the thought patterns have shifted into self-doubt and inadequacy to move this person away from the situation and into a more familiar, comfortable one. Again, we see the program trying to create self-sabotaging thoughts and behaviors.

Core factors to address: Value-proposition (self-value, self-worth) as well as a program that requires that he work for his value; avoidance (wanting to avoid the pain or discomfort by withdrawing or retreating)

After examining these intrusive thought patterns, we can see that he has a major struggle with the value proposition. He doesn't believe in himself despite his current level of success. Many times, we tend only to see through the lens of our emotions when we're struggling, even if our external circumstances prove otherwise. This brought a lot of negative self-reflection in his abilities to succeed and reach his goals. He doesn't feel as if he fits the idea of what he thinks he should be to reach the level of success he desires. This shows us that he has unrealistic or distorted ideas of the standard that he should meet but doesn't.

The belief that he must work for his value is one that doesn't serve him well because if he fails to meet the expectations he has placed on himself, he will reinforce the belief that he isn't good enough. This is a very common belief that many people have and is one that I had for most of my life. The problem with this belief is that when people do not produce the ideal results they want, they begin to question and label themselves in a negative way, which reinforces the program of not being valuable enough. They are basing their internal value on their external results. External results will always fluctuate and change. Your value as a person will not. Once we were able to identify this core issue, we worked to create a new understanding of his value. Now he recognizes the truth that his value never changes and is independent from his work and results. This also allowed him to work on facing his pain and discomfort instead of running. He began to recognize his ability to get through anything that comes his way in life, so he allowed himself to face and overcome those fears and pain so he could move forward and create greater levels of success.

## Fear-Based Intrusive Thoughts

I included a separate section for fear-based intrusive thoughts to demonstrate how the ITI process can work the same with them as it can with any other intrusive thought pattern to relieve fears since anxiety is directly related to them. Though fears are not the same issue as phobias and there can be a different process for working through them, this process can also be very beneficial in working through and resolving them. Phobias are typically more extreme and paralyzing, and some require a one-on-one approach to overcome them.

Fear is a common problem that can be extremely debilitating when it becomes a large part of someone's thought processes. Fear is not necessarily a bad thing, as it can provide us with hypervigilance that is useful in times of danger or caution. However, when applied to life in areas where there is no real danger or in an exaggerated way that doesn't serve you well and causes you to become paralyzed or immobile, it's time to address those fears and thought patterns so you can enjoy a greater sense of freedom and security. Fear is one of the primary driving forces that keep most people stuck or from reaching their goals. When we let fear guide or control our lives, we develop unhealthy, debilitating struggles. Fear can keep you stuck where you are, cause you to behave in harmful or destructive ways, keep you from chasing your goals and dreams, or even push you into deeper levels of anxiety and depression.

The root cause of fear is a lack of psychological security, which can cause many dysfunctional behaviors based on how it affects your psyche. The foundation for psychological security typically comes from the father figure in your life as you grow up, but this may not be the case for everyone. If you experience a lot of fear in your life, then it's time to begin rebuilding your foundation of psychological security. You must go inside to perform this job. By laying a stronger, more effective foundation of psychological security in the subconscious mind, you will build your resilience and manage life situations more effectively.

This was a struggle I experienced in my life for over thirty years, causing me to sabotage myself in many ways, personally and professionally, and leading to many regrets, poor decisions, and broken relationships with people I cared for deeply. When I recognized this issue within myself through some exercises I completed in some of my studies, I immediately went to work rebuilding my foundation of security. Now I acknowledge my resilience and ability to bounce back from struggles more than ever, and it's rare for circumstances or situations to knock me off my game. This took some time for me, as it will for you. Remember, everything follows the law of process. Using the ITI process has been a powerful tool that has helped me get where I am, and I continue to use it to stay healthy. Let's examine the ITI process with fear-based intrusive thoughts.

**Example:** This example comes from a young woman I worked with who struggled with relationship fears. She had been in a few relationships where she noticed a pattern of retreating when she became too deeply involved. She said she would become bored with the guy after some time and push him away. She didn't understand why she continued to repeat this pattern. She was active in her faith as a Christian and decided that she wanted to wait until marriage to have sexual intercourse. She was in her mid-twenties and had learned to guard herself in such a way that she wouldn't let people in or trust very easily.

**Step I:** The first step is to become aware of and identify the fear-based intrusive thoughts and feelings you are experiencing at the moment about this subject.

*What fear-based intrusive thoughts and feelings are you experiencing?*

1. **I'm never going to find the right guy.**
2. **If I do open myself up fully, he may reject me.**
3. **I may get bored with him and be unhappy.**
4. **He may only want me for my money.**
5. **A guy my age won't be willing to abstain from sex.**
6. **Maybe I'm not worth waiting for.**
7. **Maybe I'm just destined to be alone forever.**

**Step II: Truth**

Now that you've exhausted all fear-based intrusive thoughts and feelings, it's time to evaluate each of them by breaking them down with probing questions to discover the truth and lies that are driving them. The key here is to question everything in the breakdown process to uncover all lies. Once you have completed that, write out your truth statement.

1. **I'm never going to find the right guy.** *Is this statement true? Are you "never" going to find the right guy?* **I do think I'll find the right guy for me when the time is right. I guess I'm just frustrated because I haven't had the best experiences in my**

past relationships and I feel as if I can't seem to get it right with guys. *I understand. Just because you've had some past relationships that didn't work, does that mean that it will always be that way for you?* No. *What will you do if you don't find the right guy?* I'll get through it and figure it out, just as I always have.

*What is the truth?* Things can change. I do believe I'll find the right guy when the timing is right. And whether I do or not, I will get through it and be okay, just as I always have been and am now.

2.  If I do open myself up fully, he may reject me. *Is this statement true? If you open yourself up to someone, is there a chance he will reject you?* Sure, there's always that chance. *Is it okay to be rejected?* Yes. It's not what I want, but it is okay. I've been rejected before, and I'm doing pretty well now, so I guess if it happens again in the future, I will be okay then as well. *If you never fully open yourself up to someone, can they fully accept you?* No. *So would it be correct to say that your fear of rejection is keeping you from allowing yourself to be accepted?* Yes.

    *What is the truth?* There's always a chance of rejection from others, but if I don't allow myself to be open to someone, I will never be fully accepted. Taking the risk of being rejected by being open is worth the price of gaining a lifelong partner.

3.  I may get bored with him and be unhappy. *Is this statement true? Is it possible that you may become bored in a relationship?* Yes, it's possible. *Is that okay for you to experience?* Yes. It's not what I want, but it is okay. *What will you do if you become bored?* I can leave the relationship and find one that is better for me. *Can a relationship create or determine your happiness in life?* No. It can affect my happiness, but it doesn't create or define it.

*What is the truth?* It is possible that I could become bored in a relationship or that it may not be one that I'm happy with. If that's the case, I can always choose to step out of the relationship and find another partner I feel better being with.

4. He may only want me for my money. *Is this statement true? Is it possible that someone will only want you for your money?* Yeah, it's possible. *What can you do if this happens?* I can walk away from the relationship.

   *What is the truth?* Someone may only want me for my money. If this happens, I am not stuck with them. I can walk away from that relationship.

5. A guy my age won't be willing to abstain from sex. *Is this statement true? Will a guy your age not be willing to abstain from sex?* No. Most guys wouldn't be willing, but some would be willing to abstain.

   *What is the truth?* There are guys out there that would be willing to abstain from sex. I'm not the only one who wants to wait or has the beliefs I have about sex and marriage.

6. Maybe I'm not worth waiting for. *Is this statement true? Are you not worth waiting for?* No. I am worth waiting for.

   *What is the truth?* I am worth waiting for, and the guy I'm supposed to be with will be willing to wait for me.

7. Maybe I'm just destined to be alone forever. *Is this statement true? Are you destined to be alone forever?* I don't know what my destiny is, but I don't believe I'm destined to be alone forever. *What if you are destined to be alone forever, then what will you do?* I guess I'll figure it out. *Will you be okay if that's your destiny?* Yes. It's not what I want, but I'll be okay if that's my destiny.

*What is the truth?* I don't know what my destiny is or what the future holds, but either way I know I will be okay and things will work out for me the way they are supposed to.

## Step III: Insight

Now it's time to evaluate the previous steps to gain insight into your fears, why they are there, and how they are affecting you. This step is the same for gaining insight as the previous techniques I have shared through PTIR and ITI. The insight I am sharing is not the only insight into these statements. You may see some things that stick out to you that I do not mention. The objective is to understand the systems and programs driving them so you can work on and heal them.

1. **I'm never going to find the right guy. This statement shows a lack of confidence or belief in the self to have or achieve her desires. This deals with the value proposition. This is a blanket statement that shows that she is projecting her future based on her past, which keeps the door of opportunity to create and experience a new and better future shut or less likely to happen. This type of thinking increases the possibility of recreating the same or similar experiences regarding her relationships in the future. As with most fears, we can see that her foundation of security has been damaged through painful experiences and will need some work to rebuild a healthy one. This is when we look to the Model of Power to understand that her mental state is future and past based. To open herself up to new experiences and opportunities, I helped her refocus her mental state into the present and reminded her of her resilience and ability to experience a change in this area of her life.**

2. **If I do open myself up fully, he may reject me. This statement shows a low-value proposition and that she has identified with past negative experiences. Not opening herself up to others through vulnerability shows that she may feel that she isn't**

good enough for someone to choose to be with her. Many people do not open themselves up fully to their partners, which can cause problems in their relationships. This is a defense mechanism she uses to protect herself from getting hurt, but it is actually what continues to cause her pain.

3. I may get bored with him and be unhappy. This statement shows a cycle of searching outside of herself for happiness. Many people who tend to seek thrills and rely on their feelings to dictate what they do in life become discontent with what they have very quickly. There are many reasons for this, but we can see through this statement that she relies on her external environment to supply or feed her internal needs.

4. He may only want me for my money. This statement shows a low-value proposition. Something within is telling her that her monetary value is higher than her personal worth and that someone may value and want her money more than her. This program tells her that she doesn't have enough value to give someone on her own and that money may be the primary motive for someone deciding to stick it out with her.

5. A guy my age won't be willing to abstain from sex. This statement reveals a low-value proposition that tells her that she can't have what she wants unless she compromises her spiritual beliefs. She is used to setting herself up for failure through expectations she cannot reach, which is causing her to believe she cannot reach this one as well. As strange as it may sound, this program is designed to reinforce that she is not good enough and can't have what she wants in life. This also reveals a lower level of psychological security that tells her that she won't be able to sustain such a relationship without giving in.

6. Maybe I'm not worth waiting for. This statement shows a low-value proposition that causes her to feel as if she is not

valuable enough for someone to be willing to wait for her or
that what she is willing to offer isn't enough for someone else.

7. Maybe I'm just destined to be alone forever. This statement
shows a low-value proposition. This idea is designed to keep
her from moving forward by holding herself back from trying
or pursuing a relationship. This is her defense mechanism of
avoidance and withdrawal designed to keep her safe.

**Core factors to address: Value-proposition, avoidance (running from
discomfort and struggle), psychological security**

As we examine these fears and gain insight as to why she has them, we
can see a few of the core issues for her to address. First and foremost
is the value proposition. As I have stated many times, the value a
person feels they have will be at the core of almost everything they
do. When the value proposition is low, people become dysfunctional
and create cycles in their lives that can be destructive or debilitating
as a way to overcompensate for what they believe they lack. This is
the very first place to begin working on and healing. It affected her
confidence and psychological security, keeping her from being happy.
We can also recognize that she has a defense mechanism that influences
her to withdraw or avoid things that she feels may be uncomfortable.
Understanding this is helpful because when she became aware of this,
she was able to manage it and change the response when it kicked in as
she worked through these issues. She showed signs of setting herself up
for failure by holding herself to standards and expectations she typically
cannot reach. This reveals a program within her designed to keep her
where she is through self-sabotage. This primarily comes from the low-
value proposition but should be addressed as a separate issue.

# CHAPTER 13

# HEALING CORE ISSUES

As you work through the problems and intrusive thoughts using the tools and techniques I have shared with you, you will start to notice recurring core issues and themes in each one. They may express themselves differently in different areas of your life, but certain core issues will typically affect many or even all areas of your life in different ways. One of the most common is the value proposition. When you have a low self-esteem or value system, it will affect almost every area of your life and the choices you make for yourself. What I have found extremely helpful for myself and others is to create truth cards to read just after awaking in the mornings, throughout the day as needed, and before going to bed at night. Remember, one of the ways the brain learns is through repetition. Creating truth cards can help you implement the changes you desire by continually pushing in the truths you discover through the breakdown processes you learned.

To create truth cards that will help you heal the core issues, look for recurring themes in your breakdown processes—such as the value proposition, confidence issues, psychological security, and so forth—and write down the truths you have discovered on a card or notepad so you can read it regularly to reprogram your mind and rebuild those foundational programs and belief systems in your subconscious mind. Let's see what this would look like using the examples from the discernment processes, PTIR, and ITI processes explained earlier. As you read each set of truths, notice how empowering these statements are. Each of them is in-line with truth and ultimately brings the personal power and responsibility back to the individual to make more effective decisions in this area of their life that, when repeated each day, will effectively reprogram the mind to respond accordingly.

## Discernment Process I
### Example I

- The truth is, I do want to take care of my body in a healthy way.
- The truth is, I do want to eat and drink healthily.
- The truth is, I do enjoy taking care of my body.
- The truth is, I can overcome any feeling or emotion I experience while staying healthy in my habits.
- The truth is, I am in control, and no food or beverage is more powerful than I am.
- The truth is, I can do this. It is my choice, and I am responsible for my actions and behaviors.

### Example II

- The truth is, giving in to my feelings and the lies that tell me I want to be inactive creates more discomfort and pain in my life.
- The truth is, I do want to be active and outgoing, and I can be.
- The truth is, I do like being active and outgoing.
- The truth is, being active and outgoing makes me feel good, and I am happier when I am.
- The truth is, I am in control of my feelings and emotions.
- The truth is, I can take responsibility for my life right now and experience it in a greater, more fulfilling way as well as reach my goals. It is my choice.

## Discernment Process II
### Example I

- The truth is, it is okay for me to take care of myself the way I need to first. By doing so, I can take better care of all the things and people I am responsible for in my life.
- The truth is, doing what's right for me is okay.

- The truth is, I am not responsible for other people's feelings or experiences. My job is to make sure my intentions are in-line with my values.
- The truth is, it is okay for someone else to not like or approve of my decisions. This has nothing to do with me, nor is it any of my business.
- The truth is, I am a great person. This is not dependent on someone else thinking this. It depends on me.
- The truth is, my mother's feelings, actions, and behaviors are not a reflection of me but of her.

## Example II

- The truth is, I am always where I'm supposed to be. It is okay for me to be where I am, at all times.
- The truth is, I can have all the things I want in life.
- The truth is, it's not my job to be like everyone else, just me.
- The truth is, being who I am, doing what I am doing, and being where I am in life has nothing to do with anyone else. This applies to everyone else as well.
- The truth is, I am valuable no matter what I do, have done, or will do in my life. This will never change.
- The truth is, everything is part of the divine plan and there is no plan for me other than the divine plan.
- The truth is, I am on my path, and it's the right path for me. I don't have to let others' expectations control me or what I do. This is my life and my responsibility, nobody else's.

## Discernment Process III
### Example I

- The truth is, I am not stuck where I currently am in life. I can choose to take greater responsibility for my health by eating healthily and exercising.
- The truth is, it is okay to be where I am in this process as I work toward a more desirable outcome.

- The truth is, the weight of my body has nothing to do with my character or value.
- The truth is, I can change my results by taking steps today.
- The truth is, I can refocus my mind toward a healthier lifestyle.
- The truth is, I want to eat healthier and exercise because I want to take care of my body.
- The truth is, I can do this. I can release this extra weight because I do have a choice.
- The truth is, I am a hardworking person, and I know how to get things done. It's part of who I am.

Example II

- The truth is, I am valuable. Nothing can change this. My value as a person doesn't depend on my physical capabilities.
- The truth is, I have much to offer others in life, such as love, kindness, patience, and compassion. These are the greatest gifts I could ever give to someone else, and they have nothing to do with my physical capabilities.
- The truth is, I am blessed to have someone willing and able to help me when I need it.
- The truth is, I deserve to have the help I have from my wife and others. If I didn't deserve it, I wouldn't have it.
- The truth is, I am a blessing to others.
- The truth is, it is okay to need help. All people need help at some point in their lives. I am no exception to this. It doesn't make others a burden or worthless, nor does it make me a burden or worthless.
- The truth is, what I am and am not capable of doing during this time in my life is perfectly okay.

PTIR
Example I

- The truth is, trusting people is a good thing and a great quality to have.

- The truth is, I want to and can have friends in my life that are healthy for me.
- The truth is, sometimes people come and go in life. This happens for a purpose, and this is okay.
- The truth is, my past doesn't have to dictate my future. I can make new choices and experience new things in my life as I choose. I can choose to release my past right now by living in the present moment and beginning to create a new and better future for myself.
- The truth is, I am a very intelligent person. I am also still learning life as it flows, and this is okay. I will make mistakes because I am human. This has nothing to do with my level of intelligence.
- The truth is, my value has nothing to do with anyone else. I am valuable and deserving of having the things in my life that I desire.
- The truth is, there are many people around me that I care for and who care for me. If I didn't deserve it, then I wouldn't have it.
- The truth is, I am a good person. I have great morals and values, I'm a fun person to be around, and I have much to offer in this world.
- The truth is, I can make good decisions and trust myself to do what is right for me. I will make mistakes because that's part of being human and learning lessons, and that has nothing to do with my ability to make good decisions.
- The truth is, by loving and taking care of myself, I will create an environment that supports better and more fulfilling relationships with others that are healthy for me.

Example II

- The truth is, being fully me and authentic is what I want to be and what I should be. Being me is what's right and best for me.
- The truth is, I am most valuable as myself. This does not depend on or have anything to do with anyone else's opinions

or expectations. If I were supposed to be like someone else, I would be. I'm me, and that's the best thing I can be.

- The truth is, I like being me and how I am. It is okay for others to disagree with this, but that's within them. I can choose to stand in my power by being authentic and focusing on living my own life the way I see fit.
- The truth is, it's my job and responsibility to be who I am. I have great gifts and talents that are unique to me because I am unique. This is part of what makes me who I am. To take my uniqueness away for the sake of anyone else's expectations does not serve me well. And I want to be served well by my actions and behaviors.
- The truth is, I can choose to take responsibility for my thought patterns, emotional states, and actions, and align them with love, compassion, peace, and harmony. This is what I genuinely want to do.
- The truth is, I am not responsible for anyone else's opinions, expectations, or experiences. I am only responsible for my intentions and myself.

## ITI
Example I

- The truth is, I am fully capable of achieving my goals. I do have what it takes. I've reached many goals in my life because I can do so.
- The truth is, I am valuable and good enough. Nothing I do or do not do can change this. My value is not a product of my results in life. It is a product of my being.
- The truth is, I do belong.
- The truth is, I am a good person. I may have made mistakes in my past, but I have learned from them.
- The truth is, I do deserve to be successful. I work very hard and am a person of integrity. I can and I will create success in my life.

- The truth is, I am smart, hardworking, worthy, and capable of performing at higher levels and being as successful as I desire.

**Fear-Based ITI**
**Example**

- The truth is, I am worthy and deserving of having a great partner in life. I have so much love to offer and give.
- The truth is, there's nothing wrong with wanting what I want. There are others out in this world who have the same or similar beliefs and attract their soul mates. I can do the same.
- The truth is, I am worth waiting for, and the person I choose to be with will be lucky and blessed to have me in their life.
- The truth is, I am valuable. My current situation doesn't define my value. I am where I am supposed to be at this moment in my life, and it's okay for me to be here.
- The truth is, I am more than enough on my own for the person I am meant to be with.

You can write down on your truth card many different truths. These are only examples of how to write a truth card in such a way to reprogram your mind and align your thoughts with truth for a better, more effective outcome. When you repeat these truths daily, after some time you will notice your thought patterns beginning to shift and align with them automatically. This happens when you start to replace the old belief systems with new ones that will change the experiences and outcomes you create in your life. Keep in mind the process of the reticular activating system, which primarily responds to the emotional states by repeating your truths with positive emotion. This can help drive them deeper into the mind for quicker programming. You can use each card for as long as you desire, and you can make as many truth cards as you'd like. I have several that I read at different times to help me stay balanced and empowered.

# Mirror Technique

The Mirror Technique is powerful and can help drive your truths deeper and much faster. You may have heard of this technique from many other people prominent in the world of self-help, such as Jack Canfield and Tony Robbins. I have used this great technique for many years to help me create significant change, and I highly recommend it. There are many different variations of the mirror technique, but I'm going to teach you the method I use and how to perform it most effectively to bring more significant results in a shorter amount of time. The mirror technique is a conscious process of reprogramming the subconscious mind through talking with yourself while standing in front of a mirror and staring at your reflection. Since we understand that change must take place in the subconscious mind, we want to perform this in such a way that it allows us to reach the subconscious mind while in a conscious state. We have three primary means of taking in information: sight, sound, and feeling. We want to utilize each of these senses in the mirror technique for the most effectiveness. Performing this technique is extremely easy, but it can be a bit tedious because you have to stand or sit for several minutes while in front of a mirror. Nevertheless, it can be a potent tool to boost your growth quickly. Let's examine the steps and how to perform the mirror technique in the way I have found most beneficial and effective.

**Step I:** **Stand in front of a mirror that reflects your body from the waist up**

If you don't have a mirror that reflects from the waist up, you can use a full-length mirror or one that shows from the chest up. If you cannot stand for long periods comfortably, you can sit in front of a mirror and receive the same results from this technique.

**Step II:** **Assume the posture technique and stare at your dominant eye**

Imagine for a moment that standing in front of you is the version of yourself that is disempowered, fearful, lacking confidence, and just beaten down by life. What would your body posture look like? Your head would probably be pointing toward the floor. Your shoulders would probably be slumped over, and your back may be slouching. You inherently know this already because of the connection between your body and brain.

Now imagine standing in front of you is the version of yourself that is empowered, confident, happy, and ready for whatever comes your way in life. What would your body posture look like now? Your head would be straight up, eyes wide open, shoulders erect, and your back straight. This is the posture technique (sometimes referred to as the superman technique.) This is important because as you focus visually on your dominant eye (once you start focusing on your eyes, you will notice your focus shifting toward your dominant eye), your brain waves will begin to slow down and move into an alpha brain wave state. This is the lightest trance state of hypnosis, which we call self-hypnosis. When you're in this trance state, all signals will go directly to your subconscious mind. You will be sending a visual message and image to your subconscious mind that you are confident, ready, capable, happy, and standing in your power. Remember, the mind can't tell the difference between real and imagined.

**Step III: Begin making these statements to yourself aloud while adding positive emotions and feeling them as deeply as you can**

1. I am proud of you for ...

   These statements will boost your self-confidence and value proposition in many ways. Repeat this phrase and things you are proud of yourself for doing or achieving. This doesn't just apply to the big achievements you've had in your life but rather anything you can think of (such as getting out of bed on time, managing your priorities more effectively, making a difficult decision, and so on). The purpose is to begin rebuilding your sense of self-worth and self-power. Before you know it, you'll be proclaiming how proud you are to yourself and others without even thinking about it.

2.  I forgive you for ...

    This statement will allow you to heal and move forward from things and mistakes you have beat yourself up over. Forgiveness is a powerful force that—when implemented into your life—can create great peace and allow you to create new experiences in your life.

3.  I love you because ...

    This statement is all about self-love. Loving and nurturing yourself is one of the most effective and essential actions you can take in your life. This will enhance your mental, emotional, spiritual, and physical health. You will begin taking better care of and showing compassion to yourself once this begins to work its way into your subconscious mind.

4.  Truth Statements

    This is where your truth statements come in. This does require that you begin to memorize your truth statements or other affirmations you decide to use. However, don't wait until you have memorized them to start using this technique. If you haven't learned or know them by heart, tape or mount them somewhere in front of you and read them out loud. Be sure to remain in the posture technique and return your focus to your dominant eye as much as possible. Even if you are not consciously focused on your dominant eye while you are reading your truths, your subconscious mind can still see the visual you are presenting with the posture technique through your peripheral. Since your truth statements are already set and structured, you'll want to repeat them from beginning to end over and over until you have satisfied whatever time you have decided to invest in that session. It doesn't matter

**whether you make "I" statements or "you" statements when reciting your truth statements as they are both effective.**

Remember, one of the ways the brain learns new information is through repetition so when you're repeating that you are proud of yourself, you forgive yourself, and that you love yourself, you are developing a deeper sense of healthy pride, forgiveness, and self-love. When you make each of these statements, add as much positive emotion to it as you can muster up. This is important because of the reticular activating system that responds to higher emotional attachments and states. While performing this technique, you may hear all kinds of dialogue in your mind telling you that you're not this or that or in some way trying to convince you that what you are saying is wrong. Don't worry too much about this. It's quite normal at first. Once you have been doing this technique for a few weeks, those voices and thoughts will dissipate.

**Step IV: Smile at yourself for one minute**

For some, this can be an awkward experience at first. Some people don't like their smiles or they have issues with their complex, so they don't enjoy this step much. This is even more reason to perform it. When you take the last minute to smile at yourself, you are sending the signal to your mind that you are happy. When the mind perceives you as happy, you will create more happiness in your life.

The mirror technique is very simple but powerful in helping create positive change in your life. Beware of the terror barrier as you begin to implement this. Many people start to lose interest and motivation after a few weeks. This is where it becomes a bit tedious and people get out of their routine. Do your best to stay focused and push through the discomfort and self-sabotage when it arises, and it will. When you perform this technique, do so with enthusiasm, passion, and excitement. At first, you may not feel very comfortable. You must overlook these feelings. Once you become familiar with and comfortable doing this, those feelings will fade away.

Remember the law of process. Do not expect immediate results with this or any other technique. It requires consistency and dedication. I recommend starting with five minutes in the beginning, and once you become used to doing this, extend your time to whatever feels comfortable to you. Based on my personal experience, I have found that ten minutes is the optimal time frame for me. When you are in a trance state, time will become distorted, so I recommend setting a timer on your phone or another device to help you keep track of it. I also recommend doing this technique at least once per day for a minimum of thirty days. Doing this in the morning before beginning your day is a great way to start with a more positive mindset, which can lead to greater experiences throughout the day. Performing this technique just before going to bed at night is very powerful as well because the programming will make its way into the subconscious mind as you fall asleep. I encourage you to explore this technique and find the way that suits you best.

## Meditation

This book wouldn't be complete if I didn't touch on a practice that is so beneficial and powerful for creating change. Meditation is a practice that has been passed down for thousands of years for a good reason. Meditation is such an important practice to implement, as it can bring greater awareness and peace into your life. Many people become discouraged because they can't seem to clear their minds while sitting still. They think it's a waste of time to sit with a full mind. It's not. Having a full mind as you meditate doesn't mean you've wasted your time or that you weren't successful. It can be just as effective as sitting with a clear mind.

To meditate means to become familiar with the self. When you sit down to meditate, do so with a curious mind. Let go of any agenda you may have and take what's called the "witness stand." This means to be curious to learn more about the self. Instead of trying to control your thoughts, just become aware of them without any attachment. Using the same principle of shifting your mind to the present state can help you achieve this during meditation sessions. Developing a daily practice of meditation can help you become more grounded, centered, and help you manage your emotions more effectively. There are also many added benefits emotionally, mentally, spiritually, and physically.

It's important to understand that meditation alone will not get rid of your anxiety or depression, but it can help you manage it more effectively as you work through the processes you have learned in this book. There are many others out there with greater knowledge and understanding of meditation than myself, and I encourage you to seek them out if you want to learn more about meditation, but I will teach you my method, which may help you begin your journey. I like to use neurofeedback and biofeedback to help me stay focused and track my progress as I meditate and bring my heart into coherence. Several tools out there can assist you with this if you are looking to make this a practice in your life and use science to track your progress. Here are a few simple steps to get you started on your meditation journey.

**Step I:** **Find a quiet space, sit in a relaxed position, and close your eyes**

It's essential to find a space where you will not be disturbed and to silence any distractions, such as your phone, when you meditate. To meditate effectively is to remain consciously aware. Sit upright or at a slight incline when meditating. When you lie down, close your eyes, and relax, you are telling your body that it is time to move into sleep mode. Your body is used to this each night as you go to sleep, so it's trained to perform this way. Sitting up can help you avoid this issue. When you first begin a meditation practice, you may find yourself occasionally falling in and out of consciousness. This is okay. I recommend starting with short time increments of five minutes and working your way up to longer sessions.

**Step II:** **Begin to focus on breathing in and out through your heart in a steady, consistent rhythm**

When you focus on the area of your chest around your heart as you breathe in and out at a slow, steady pace, you will begin to create heart coherence, which will raise your body's vibration to a state of peace and calm. Imagine breathing in and out through your heart and maintain your focus there. This will also bring your brain waves down to a calmer state. You will lose your focus at times, and that's okay. When you become aware of it, simply allow that to be okay and shift your attention back to your heart region as you slowly inhale and exhale. You don't have to take deep breaths—just slow, consistent breaths. This is also a powerful way of relieving stress without meditating, which I highly recommend anytime you feel worked up or negative.

That's all you need to do to begin a practice of meditation. A very simple and effective practice, it can shift your reality significantly and help you achieve a higher state of peace and happiness in your life as you outgrow anxiety and depression. You can easily find guided meditation sessions on YouTube and the internet that are free and well put together. I encourage you to begin a practice of meditation so you can receive the powerful benefits it has to offer. The benefits of meditation are not instantaneous. Everything, including meditation, follows the law of process, so don't expect immediate results. Give yourself at least thirty days and then reflect on the benefits you notice.

## Diet and Exercise

Reprogramming the mind is necessary to overcome anxiety and depression, but research has shown that gut health can also be a contributing factor for many people. It's important to understand that there is a mind-body connection where they both support each other. Taking care of your body is all about self-care and self-love. Loving yourself is necessary when working to change your life for the better. To truly have a healthy mind, you must take care of your body in a healthy way. The most effective way to do this is through proper nutrition. Make sure you are taking care of your body by eating foods that support you in your journey of health and well-being. If you are consuming large amounts of processed sugar or foods that break down your immune system, you are not supporting the brain in the ways that are most beneficial to help you live your life as an empowered person. Begin to incorporate some healthy meals and nutrition in your daily diet that will support your mind and body to function the way you want. Use the process of discernment to help you with this.

If you're not physically active, I highly suggest you begin an exercise or workout routine in your life. You don't have to go to a gym and work out for an hour every day. You can begin by taking walks or doing some stretching just to get started with a routine. Many people try to go all in when they begin a new diet or exercise routine, but it may be more beneficial to make small changes to begin. Once you establish a pattern or habit, you can expand to different exercises or approaches to help you progress further.

Another beneficial approach is to make a start/stop list. This is where you decide to start doing one thing to improve your health each week and stop doing one thing each week that keeps you from reaching your goals and becoming healthier. As you take steps to implement a healthier lifestyle, remember, this is an act of love and compassion toward yourself and is necessary for the process of healing. You deserve to be loved, you deserve to feel good physically and mentally, and the truth is that you want to.

## Ending the Cycles

Patience, practice, and consistency are crucial to overcoming anxiety and depression. These things can be challenging to sustain when you're in pain and suffering, but if you want to rid yourself of these debilitating experiences, you *must*. You are fighting for your life, and it's a fight worth fighting. I know how difficult changing can be, but I also know how wonderful it is to finally overcome those battles and experience true freedom, love, and peace. You must be diligent and strategic in this battle if you want to win. You must be consistent and tenacious as you work through the issues, knowing that one day you will be free from them.

I've been using these tools and techniques for a few years now, and I still work to maintain my growth. Once you have worked out many of the core issues causing most of your pain and suffering, you will find that the work becomes easier and very manageable. It's essential to remember that the pain you are experiencing from anxiety and depression will not go away on its own. You must do the work. Drugs, medications, and supplements only work to help you with the symptoms. Some people think time will heal them, but it's not time's job to heal you—it's yours. Begin to fight back by taking greater levels of responsibility for yourself and taking whatever time is necessary to do the work to eradicate anxiety and depression from your life for good.

Don't be fooled by your feelings any longer. As I said before, I want you to go and do what you want in life but realize that you will not always feel like doing it. Do the work even if you don't feel like it. You will be so glad you did. I wish you peace, love, happiness, and freedom on your path to recovery.

# BIBLIOGRAPHY

Burns, David D. *Feeling Good: The New Mood Therapy* (New York: Harper, 1992).

Burns, David D. *The Feeling Good Handbook* (New York: Plume Books, 1999).

# ABOUT THE AUTHOR

Mike Oglesbee is transformative coach and personal growth teacher who has been helping people eradicate anxiety and depression and live more effective lives since 2011, when he founded Maximized Mind, LLC, in Myrtle Beach, South Carolina. His diverse, unique background and experience with anxiety and depression, both personally and professionally, have led him to create a powerful system and philosophy that addresses the root causes of these debilitations. One of his main philosophies is that empowerment is the key to overcoming anxiety and depression, as well as most things in life. Empowerment comes through knowledge, and knowledge about the self becomes self-empowerment. Therefore, he devotes much of his time as a coach, mentor, advisor, friend, and partner to teaching and helping people understand themselves in a deeper way, allowing them to step into their own personal power and make the changes they desire in their lives.

Mike's formal educational background consists of a Bachelor of Science in psychology from the University of Phoenix and an MBA from Trident University International. He has received numerous certifications and training through several organizations and academies as a clinical hypnotherapist, neurolinguistic programming (NLP) practitioner, and life coach.

Mike has been featured on ABC television shows; numerous radio programs, including international radio; and has been featured in magazines and publications several times for his success stories.